THE CUT AND ENGRAVED GLASS OF CORNING 1868-1940

Jane Shadel Spillman
Estelle Sinclaire Farrar

The Corning Museum of Glass
Corning, New York · 1977

COPYRIGHT 1977
THE CORNING MUSEUM OF GLASS
CORNING, NEW YORK 14830

Printed in U.S.A.
Standard Book Number 0-87290-064-9
Library of Congress Catalog Card Number 77-73626
Design : Richard Erlanger

Lenders to the Exhibition

Mrs. Susan Egginton Altonen, Corning, New York
Arkansas Commemorative Commission, Little Rock,
    Arkansas
Mrs. Grace Nitsche Barker, Corning, New York
Miss Frances Barrett, Corning, New York
Mrs. Adeline Stage Butla, Lawrenceville, Pennsylvania
Mrs. Matthew M. Cammen, Corning, New York
Carnegie Institute, Museum of Art, Pittsburgh,
    Pennsylvania
Mrs. Dorothy Kaulfuss Coats, Painted Post, New York
Mrs. Jennifer Jacoby Dawson, Painted Post, New York
Mrs. Catherine Haselbauer Dencenburg, Dundee, New
    York
Mr. and Mrs. Jay Doros, Irvington, New Jersey
Mrs. Virginia Illig Driscoll, Corning, New York
Miss Evelyn and Miss Mildred Durkin, Corning, New
    York
Miss Lucille Egginton, Corning, New York
Miss Florence and Miss Evelyn Eick, Corning, New York
Mrs. Helen Libisch Elmer, Corning, New York
Mrs. Estelle Sinclaire Farrar, Garden City, New York
Carl U. Fauster, Toledo, Ohio
Mrs. Louise H. Hallahan, Corning, New York
Mrs. June Dorflinger Hardy, New York, New York
Mrs. Penrose Hawkes, Corning, New York
Milton Hershey School, Hershey, Pennsylvania
The Historical Society of Western Pennsylvania,
    Pittsburgh, Pennsylvania
Mrs. John S. Hoare, Wellsboro, Pennsylvania
Mrs. E.J. Illig, Corning, New York
Mr. and Mrs. John Jeppson, Worcester, Massachusetts
Harry Kraut, New York, New York
Miss Mary Krebs, Corning, New York
Lightner Museum, St. Augustine, Florida
Mrs. Freda Lipkowitz, Howard Beach, New York
Mansion Museum, Oglebay Institute, Wheeling, West
    Virginia
Mr. and Mrs. John C. Marx, Corning, New York
Miss A.E. McCloskey, Corning, New York
The Metropolitan Museum of Art, New York, New York
Mrs. Percy Orr, Big Flats, New York
Mrs. Edward Owlett, Wellsboro, Pennsylvania
Mrs. Edward J. Palme, Jr., Corning, New York
Mrs. Esther Kretschmann Patch, Corning, New York
Mrs. Beatrice Perling, Elmira, New York
Philadelphia Museum of Art, Philadelphia,
    Pennsylvania
Wilmot L. Putnam, Jr., Painted Post, New York
Mr. and Mrs. Philip Roberts, Princeton, New Jersey
The Rockwell-Corning Museum, Corning, New York
Robert F. Rockwell III, Corning, New York
Mrs. Emil Schrickel, Corning, New York
Mrs. Louise Giometti Smith, Painted Post, New York
Mrs. Sheldon Smith, Summit, New Jersey
Smithsonian Institution, Washington, D.C.
Mrs. Dorothy Hunt Sullivan, Corning, New York
Leon Swope, Wellsboro, Pennsylvania
The Toledo Museum of Art, Toledo, Ohio
Museum of Glass, Wheaton Historical Association,
    Millville, New Jersey
Nicholas Williams, Corning, New York
Mrs. Phillip Willis, Rochester, New York
One anonymous lender

Table Of Contents

Foreword

Of the one hundred and twenty-seven special exhibitions presented by the Corning Museum of Glass since the first in 1951 ("A Century of Taste"), only three have focused on glass made in the city of Corning: "The Life and Work of Frederick Carder" (1952), "Asian Artists in Crystal" (1956), and "Steuben: Seventy Years of American Glassmaking" (1975). Considering the role in American history of this geographic location as a major glass manufacturing center, this is hardly a record of self aggrandizement; considering the fact that not one of the exhibitions has explored either the cutting shops or the industrial activity on which the area's glass fame rests, the record is downright misleading. With this exhibition and catalogue on cut and engraved glass in Corning, Estelle Sinclaire Farrar, an independent scholar and granddaughter of H.P. Sinclaire, Jr. (founder of one of Corning's outstanding cutting firms), and Jane Shadel Spillman, a specialist in American Glass since she came to the Museum in 1965, have joined forces to put the record in better balance and introduce us to what really happened.

The Corning Museum of Glass is a non-profit, accredited educational institution chartered by the Board of Regents of the State of New York. It was founded and has always been supported by Corning Glass Works. Although never a cutting shop itself, the Glass Works brought cutting to Corning in 1868 when it agreed to make blanks exclusively for Hoare & Dailey if they moved here too. Now, 109 years later, the arts practiced by the cutters and the engravers are very much alive in the extraordinary craftsmen working in the Steuben Division of Corning Glass Works.

Thomas S. Buechner, Director
The Corning Museum of Glass

Preface

The house was the ordinary frame dwelling of a workingman, and scores of similar homes sprawled over the side of one of the twin hills.... It was the home of a man who might earn $2. a day—enough in an upstate city like Corning to provide a large family with necessaries.... The door of the house was open ... the dining room was set for the noonday meal. Nothing strange about that. Yet there was something strange about that table. Scattered about in careless profusion, looking a little out of place on the cheap red tablecloth were pieces of cut glass—real cut glass. There was no doubting their genuineness. They gleamed with white light and prismatic color, and their facets glittered as only cut glass facets can. It was the cut glass of the sideboards and tables of the rich. And the stranger wondered how it came there—that is until he remembered that he was in Corning, the cut glass city of New York State, in which ... more high grade glass is cut each year than in any other city in the country.

This quotation, from a feature story in the November 23, 1902, issue of the *New York Sunday Tribune*, aptly underscores the reputation of the City of Corning in the cut glass industry at the turn of the century.

In preparing an exhibition to tell the story of Corning's position in this industry, it is impossible to include in this catalogue all of the available information. A comprehensive book covering the entire story of cutting and engraving in Corning will be published in the future. We have chosen here only to give an account of the contributions of the area and of the people who made the glass.

To provide a historical framework, earlier glass is included as well as glass from Corning's competitors. We are grateful to the many lenders who have entrusted their glass to the Museum and especially to those who have loaned cherished productions of their fathers and grandfathers.

Jane Shadel Spillman
Estelle Sinclaire Farrar

Cut glass floor lamp bought by Milton Hershey at the World's
Columbian Exposition, Chicago, 1893. The lamp is shown in the
Hershey home, Hershey, Pennsylvania, early in the century.
Courtesy Milton S. Hershey School

Production Methods

Glass has been cut since ancient times, but it was not until the nineteenth century that the combination of an especially suitable glass, steam power for cutting wheels, and Victorian tastes gave rise to the style called "brilliant" cut glass. The perfection of the curved cut in 1886 encouraged even more elaborate designs. Although all glass can be cut, the peculiar attributes of lead glass—its softness and its high index of refraction—make it particularly appropriate for cutting. Its softness permits it to be cut easily with less chance of breakage than a more brittle glass. Its high index of refraction causes light rays passing through the glass to be reflected as in a prism, and this gives the cutting the brilliance of diamonds.

In addition to good glass, the cutting of glass requires good workmen. In the beginning all those workmen came from Europe. The process of cutting varied little from that used in Europe in the late seventeenth century, although the gradual introduction of steam power in the nineteenth century made the work easier and permitted deeper cuts. Previously the power had been supplied by hand, usually by a helper turning a large wheel, and the speed of the cutting wheel consequently was variable. Steam power for cutting wheels was introduced in England about 1807 and was in use in Boston by 1819 at the New England Glass Company. Water power was used by some factories in England and Ireland, but there is no evidence that it was utilized in the United States.

The cutting wheel was held by an apparatus called a frame. In the early days, a cutter was forced to change his wheels when he wished to change the size or shape of his cuts, but by the end of the century some shops had more frames than cutters so that the men could move from wheel to wheel to continue work on a given piece without stopping. Early in the century a single cutter worked on each piece, but by the 1890's specialization became the rule, and, after that, men were trained to do either rough cutting, smoothing, or polishing. The *Sunday Tribune* eyewitness account of cutting in Corning in 1902 explains the process clearly:

> The plain glass, after careful inspection for flaws ... is given over to a rougher who sketches the main outlines with a gummy red fluid. Then the pattern is roughed in with iron disks kept moist with a constant dripping of sand and water .... Across the room is a long row of smoothers bending over swiftly revolving wheels of craigleith or limestone, on which water is continually dropping .... The smaller parts of the design, such as the silver diamond and tops of stars are worked out by stone wheel without previous roughing .... From the smoother's stone the glass goes to a polishing wheel of poplar wood .... which is fed with a mixture of water, pumice and rottenstone. Then brush wheels are used and a final polish given with a cork wheel moistened with putty powder or a wheel of felt. On other lathes, men are grinding stoppers into bottles, for every cut glass bottle has its own stopper just as each man has his own hat and no other will fit exactly.

Copper-wheel engraving is a different technique of decoration and is the most precise, delicate, and costly of the abrasive methods. The engraver works on the *top* surface of his glass, unlike the cutter, and often works freehand. His wheels range from the size of a pinhead to a few inches in diameter. He spends days, weeks, months, or even years on a single piece. Stone engraving is similar, but larger wheels are employed to produce deeper and more coarse engraving. Intaglio cutting imitates engraving in appearance, but the cutter looks *through* his glass and cuts its far surface. Neither stone engraving nor intaglio cutting can equal copper-wheel engraving in detail.

A cutter at work: Leonard Dow at Steuben Glass, Corning Glass Works, 1920's.

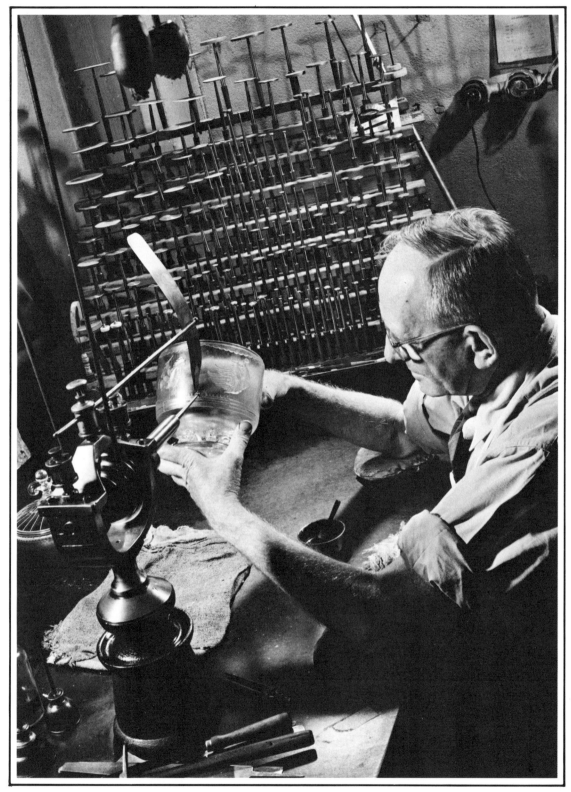

*An engraver at work: Joseph Libisch engraving the Merry-go-round
bowl, 1947. Courtesy Steuben Glass.*

Interior of the cutting room, Pairpoint Manufacturing Company, New Bedford, Massachusetts, ca. 1900.

The T.G. Hawkes & Company Showroom, Market Street, Corning, early twentieth century. Courtesy Mrs. Penrose Hawkes.

Historical Background

The roots of the American cut glass industry were established in England in the eighteenth century. Cutting as a means of decoration was in use on English glasses early in the eighteenth century and may have been introduced by the Germans who came to England in the wake of George I's accession to the throne. Cutting, however, was expensive and did not become really popular until after 1780 when the Irish Free Trade policy encouraged the movement of English glasshouses to Ireland to escape the English excise taxes on glass. These glasshouses made blown and cut wares (Figs. 1, 2), and almost all of their exports went to North America where they were copied by American cut glass manufacturers. "In the states where I have been, English tastes are prevalent in the interior of the homes, their furnishings and furniture.... In the dining room there is always a very elegant mahogany sideboard decorated with the silver...as well as with beautiful cut glass and crystal...." *(Baron Klinkowstrom's America,* 1818-1820). Mrs. Basil Hall remarked in 1827 that in homes "in the first style" at Albany, the sideboard had "beautiful china and cut glass an inch thick." From 1801 to 1812, yearly shipments of drinking glasses from Ireland to America ranged from a low of 50,000 items to a high of 370,000 in 1812 after the repeal of the Non-intercourse Act.

Little or no cut glass was made in America in the eighteenth century, although both Stiegel and Amelung produced engraved wares. A glasshouse in Kensington, near Philadelphia, advertised "plain and cut decanters" in February 1775, but nothing is known of its production. William Peter Eichbaum, a German glass cutter, arrived in Philadelphia with his family in 1793 and worked for a glass factory there, but no evidence exists to indicate whether or not it produced cut glass.

Fig. 1

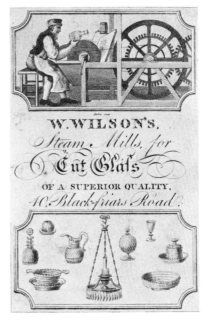

Trade Card of a cutting firm,
London, ca. 1807.

Fig. 2

13

Cutting in Nineteenth Century America
— The Midwest

Benjamin Bakewell came to Pittsburgh in 1808 and opened the first glasshouse west of the Alleghenies which produced lead glass tablewares. Pittsburgh was an ideal location for both glass and ironmakers, for there were nearby sources of fuel, and the Ohio River provided transportation. By 1809, Bakewell advertised cut glass. His glasshouse suffered from increased English competition after the close of the War of 1812. A Bakewell letter to *Niles Weekly Register*, August 30, 1819, in support of proposed tariffs, states that formerly "we gave employment to near a hundred hands and maintained about four hundred persons—at present we find it difficult to furnish the work for ten." A description of Pittsburgh's manufactories published the previous year lists eighty-two employees for the two flint glass manufacturers in the city and adds that they made glass worth $110,000. Henry Bradshaw Fearon comments in his *Sketches of America*, "I saw chandeliers and numerous articles in cut glass of a very splendid description. Among the latter was a pair of decanters cut from a London pattern, the price of which will be eight guineas...." In 1824 and 1825, Bakewell won prizes for the quality of his cut glass from the Franklin Institute in Philadelphia. At that time he employed twelve "engravers and ornamenters."

Bakewell, an Englishman, employed "excellent artists, both French and English," so it is not surprising that contemporary accounts mention that his glass was as good as English glass. Although his factory produced other kinds of glass, most of the early writers described and praised Bakewell's cut and engraved wares. The decanter (Fig. 3), with a matching celery vase, was given by the Bakewell family to Rochester, Pennsylvania, glassmaker Henry Clay Fry in 1867, although it was undoubt-

Fig. 3.

edly made around 1825. It is cut in a pattern of strawberry diamonds. Although copied from Anglo-Irish glass, this pattern has come to be called "Bakewell-type" because so much of it was made in Pittsburgh.

Bakewell made glass for a number of prominent Americans and received much public attention. In 1817 and 1829, Presidents Monroe and Jackson ordered the first American cut table services for the White House. The Monroe service is described in the local paper as "a splendid equipage of glass." The Jackson service must have been equally fine, as were the pair of vases which were presented to the Marquis de Lafayette when he made his historic visit to this country in 1824-1825. Lafayette also received a tumbler with his own likeness in the bottom. Bakewell advertised similar "cut glass tumblers, in the bottom of which, by a very ingenious process, is embedded an excellent likeness of some distinguished

American citizen, as Adams, Jackson, Lafayette &c." A tumbler with a portrait of Washington (Fig. 4) is undoubtedly one of Bakewell's products. Other tumblers with portraits of Lafayette, DeWitt Clinton, Benjamin Franklin, and Andrew Jackson are known, but none with Adams' profile has appeared so far.

Because Bakewell's factory was the largest and is the best-known today, there is a tendency on the part of collectors to attribute all Midwestern cut glass to Bakewell. It is important to remember that six other factories in Pittsburgh produced cut glass which must have been similar to Bakewell's.

John Robinson opened his Stourbridge Flint Glass Works in Pittsburgh in 1823 and soon advertised cut glass. A heavy pillar-cut decanter from this factory descended in the Robinson family until it was presented to the Historical Society of Western Pennsylvania. The cutting is quite unlike

Fig. 4

the Bakewell style of cutting and is much more like English glass of the 1840's. The Robinson glasshouse closed in 1845, and it seems likely that this decanter dates from the later years of the factory. A description of Pittsburgh in 1836 notes that the Stourbridge Flint Glass Works had eleven pots, sixty-five men and boys employed, and a steam engine of ten horsepower for the cutting of glass. About $90,000 worth of glass was produced annually at that time.

Robert Curling and William Price opened their Pittsburgh glasshouse in 1827. The cut decanter (Fig. 5), one of a pair, was a wedding gift in 1828 to Martha Curling, daughter of one of the owners. It is much simpler in style than the cut glass from either Bakewell or Robinson. Unfortunately, no other cut pieces are known from either the Robinson or Curling factories, so it is impossible to know whether they made the geometrically cut wares usually attributed to Bakewell, but it seems likely that they did.

The engraved sugar bowl (Fig. 6) is in a standard Midwestern shape and was probably engraved on a lathe powered by a foot treadle. Sugar bowls, creamers, jugs, compotes, and other tablewares with simple flower and leaf engraving were relatively common and were probably made in a number of factories in Pittsburgh and Wheeling in the second quarter of the nineteenth century.

Wheeling, a Midwestern port on the Ohio River, was an important center for early cut glass. In 1829, John Ritchie and Jesse Wheat opened a factory in Wheeling which advertised cut, pressed, and plain glass. The decanter in Figure 7 is from this factory or from its successor, which was run by the Ritchies until 1837.

The celery and salt cut in Wheeling by Michael and Thomas Sweeney's factory,

Fig. 5

1831-1848 (Figs. 8, 9), are also simply-cut pieces. In their heaviness and simple cutting, they are similar to the Robinson decanter described above. Most of the cut glass attributed to the Wheeling factories does not have the strawberry diamond cutting associated with Pittsburgh and Eastern factories. After 1850, the Wheeling and Pittsburgh factories concentrated on mass-produced tablewares and did not cut glass again in commercial quantities until the very end of the century.

Fig. 6

Fig. 7

Fig. 8

Fig. 9

Cutting in Nineteenth-Century America — The East

Glass was also cut in the major Eastern cities of Boston, New York, and Philadelphia in the nineteenth century, but these factories were started a few years later than those in the Midwest. The reason Eastern factories did not expand their cut glass market may have been explained by Fearon, who commented that "the inhabitants of Eastern America" were still importers from "the old country." An advertisement in the *Boston Daily Evening Transcript* of March 13, 1835, illustrates the availability of glass from many sources: "RICH CUT GLASS. S.A. AND W.G. Pierce have for sale the most splendid assortment of American, French and German rich and fashionable CUT GLASSWARE which can be found in this country...."

The New England Glass Company was founded in Cambridge, Massachusetts, in 1818 and two months later an article in the Boston *Commercial Gazette* stated that "...They have an establishment for Cutting Glass,...operated by Steam Power, and conducted by experienced European Glass Cutters...." From the beginning, the New England Glass Company was determined to outshine all existing factories. Examples of its work were sent to *Niles Weekly Register* for comment after a complimentary article on Bakewell glass appeared. In 1821, the "New England" cutters issued a challenge through a Providence newspaper to the cutters at George Dummer's New Jersey factory to see whose work was cut better. The result of the challenge is not known. In 1824 and 1837, the "New England" won prizes for cut glass at exhibits in Philadelphia and Boston. The decanter (Fig. 10) made for John H. Leighton, superintendent of the glasshouse from 1849 to 1874, bears his name and an engraved floral pattern as well as facet-cutting; it has the straight-sided shape common in the 1840's. Leighton's son, Henry B. Leighton, was the engraver of the ruby-cased pitcher (Fig. 11). Although the Leightons came to Cambridge from Scotland, and the form of both pitcher and decanter are English, the engraving is Germanic in style and subject. Such hunting scenes were popular subjects with Bohemian and Austrian engravers and are found throughout the nineteenth century. The Crystal Palace Exhibition of All Nations in 1851 helped spread this engraving style to England and then to the United States. Other pieces of Henry Leighton's work show the same Bohemian influence. Since Henry Leighton was born in this country, it is logical to suppose that the European-trained craftsmen at the New England Glass Company influenced his engraving.

The best-known of these European engravers was Louis Vaupel, who came to the Cambridge factory in 1852 from Germany and was supervisor of the engraving department until 1888. His goblet (Fig. 12)

Fig. 10.

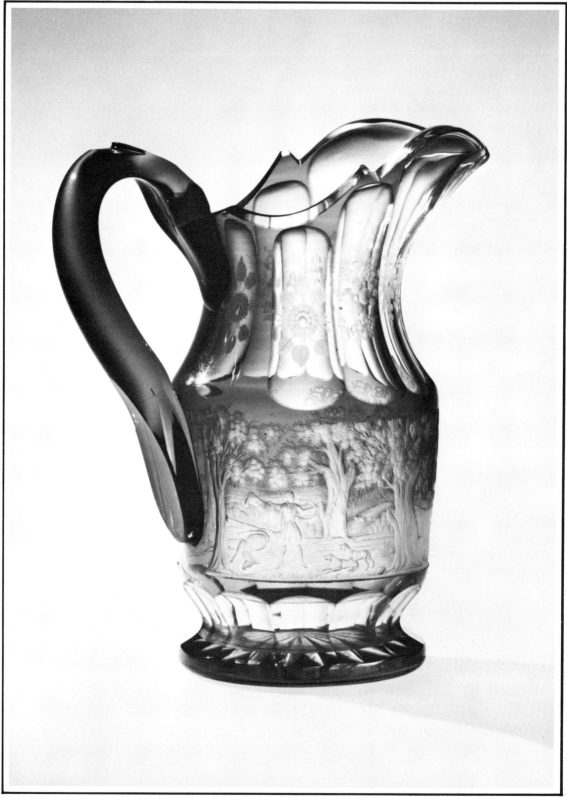

Fig. 11.

Fig. 12.

Fig. 13.

Fig. 14.

was made shortly after the Civil War. It shows an obvious resemblance in subject to Leighton's pitcher. Engraved cased glasses such as these two pieces, made of two layers of different colored glass, reached the height of their popularity in the 1850's and 1860's and are known to have been made in America at the Cambridge factory, at the Boston & Sandwich Glass Company in Sandwich, Massachusetts (founded in 1825), and at the Brooklyn Flint Glass Company, and they were probably made elsewhere as well. Objects like the Vaupel goblet and the Leighton pitcher, however, were usually special orders. The stock engraved glass was more likely to display the flowers, fruits, and initials which appear on the Leighton decanter (Fig. 10) and on the compote (Fig. 13) from the Boston & Sandwich firm. The cut compote (Fig. 14) is a New England Glass Company piece from ca. 1872-1876 and is typical of the restrained style of cutting which immediately preceded the "brilliant" period.

The engraved compote (Fig. 13) was part of a set made for William Kern in 1867 when he resigned as Boston & Sandwich factory superintendent, but it was a standard pattern which appears in an 1870's company catalogue. Another ruby overlay piece, the whiskey decanter (Fig. 15), also appears in the same catalogue and was part of Kern's gift. According to the inscription on the base, it was engraved by G.T. Lapham, who was Sandwich's best-known engraver. The cutter is unknown. The tall ruby and opaque white lamp (Fig. 16) was also made for Kern, but probably in the 1850's. The cutting on all of these pieces is fairly standard and is subordinate to the engraved decoration. The names of many engravers are known today, but the cutters remain anonymous except for those pieces which are still in the hands of descendants. After mid-century, engravers

Fig. 15.

Fig. 16.

were generally paid more than cutters.

In 1820, a group of workmen left the New England Glass Company to start a firm in Kensington, a suburb of Philadelphia. Their firm, The Union Flint Glass Company, operated for only a few years. The decanter (Fig. 17) descended in the family of Richard Synar, one of the original partners, and was one of a group of pieces attributed by family tradition to the Philadelphia firm. All are very heavy, similar in their proportions to the Ritchie pieces. The lamp (Fig. 18) is attributed to the Union factory because of the similarity of its cutting to that on a mug which also descended in the Synar family. Lamps for the parlor or dining room were often cut or engraved from the 1830's until the end of the century. The cutting on this lamp is obviously related to that on the Bakewell pieces, so a Pittsburgh origin cannot be ruled out entirely.

The glass cutting industry in New York City is not well-documented, as far as is known, but much glass was sold there throughout the nineteenth century. One of the earliest factories in the area was that of George Dummer & Co. (later P.C. Dummer & Co.), across the Hudson River in Jersey City and called the Jersey Glass Company. Dummer advertised "all kinds of cut, plain and moulded glass" and won awards for his cut glass in 1826, 1837, 1838, and 1846 at exhibits in Philadelphia and New York. Dummer's cut work was characteristically English as shown by the bowl (Fig. 19) which has the simplest possible cutting and shape and probably dates from the 1830's. With a group of other pieces, the bowl descended in the Dummer family. A green decanter set (Fig. 20) originally owned by the New York collector, Luman Reed, is also probably of Dummer's manufacture in the 1840's or from the New York Glass Works, founded in 1820 near 50th Street and 11th Avenue. The proprietors were John and Richard Fisher and John Gilliland; their factory was also called the Bloomingdale Flint Glass Works, and under that name it received a prize for the "second-best specimen of cut glass" at the Annual Fair of the American Institute of the City of New York in 1835.

Another possible source for the decanter set is the Brooklyn Flint Glass Company founded by John L. Gilliland in 1823 after he left the New York Glass Works. Gilliland also won a number of prizes for his glass and is known to have been making colored glasses in 1850. Unfortunately, no pieces which can be reliably attributed to either

Fig. 18.

Fig. 17.

Fig. 19.

Fig. 20.

the Bloomingdale or Gilliland factories are known.

The Fair of 1835, mentioned above, and the periodic exhibits at the Franklin Institute in Philadelphia, the exhibition of the Mechanics Charitable Association in Boston, and other trade fairs were all designed to display the work of American manufacturers and promote their products as comparable to those of Europe. It is difficult to distinguish between American and English cut glass until the 1890's; one reason is shown in the following advertisement:

W.R. & A.H. Sumner, No. 137 Washington Street, Boston. Cut glass. The subscribers have made arrangements to furnish sets or smaller quantities of American Glass Ware, made to order from metal of uncommon brilliancy, to match any pattern desired, whether of foreign or domestic manufacture. They have on hand, also, English Glass of the most recent patterns, and copies of the same in American Glass of a quality and style of cutting equal if not superior to that from foreign countries.
Boston Daily Journal, February 26, 1850

In the 1850's the New York City area, with an expanding and prosperous middle class, became a much more important center for the production of cut and engraved glass, perhaps because it was becoming the mercantile capital of the United States. Christian Dorflinger came from Alsace-Lorraine and started his factory on Plymouth Street, Brooklyn, in 1852. His business expanded to such an extent that he built another glasshouse on Concord Street in the late 1850's and one at Commercial Street, Greenpoint, in Brooklyn in 1860. The compote (Fig. 17) which descended in the Dorflinger family was probably made at the Plymouth Street factory around 1856 and shows the heavy simplicity of mid-century cut pieces. The ewer (Fig. 17) is not a Dorflinger family piece but is identical to one formerly owned by Miss Katherine Dorflinger, Christian's daughter. In 1861, Mary Todd Lincoln ordered a set of glassware for the White House from Dorflinger's new Greenpoint Works; the pattern combines very simple cutting with a delicate engraving of the United States coat of arms (Figs. 21, 22). At this time Dorflinger's cutting was being done by John Hoare and Joseph Dailey, who operated a shop in his factory as well as one on the premises of the Brooklyn Flint Glass Company, which had closed around 1853. Hoare had come to the United States from England, and

Fig. 21.

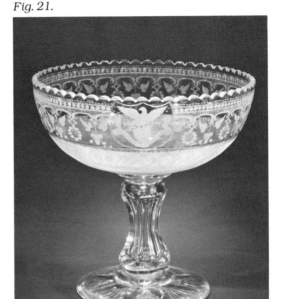

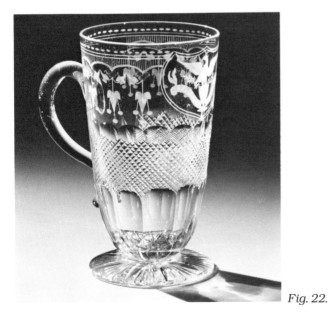

Fig. 22.

by 1857 he advertised that he had bought the cutting equipment of the Brooklyn Flint Glass Company and was prepared to serve customers at that location.

Christian Dorflinger leased his business to former employees in 1863 and moved to White Mills, Pennsylvania, where, after a few inactive years, he once more opened a glass factory. The delicate wineglass (Fig. 13 center) was made in 1869 for the wedding of his cousin, Eugene, and is in a new style, more delicate in execution and subject. The goblet (Fig. 13 left) is dated November 29, 1869, and was probably made for Mr. and Mrs. John Hoare's twenty-fifth wedding anniversary. By this time, Hoare had closed his cutting shop at the Brooklyn Flint Glass Company and moved some of his workmen to Corning to the factory of the Corning Flint Glass Company. He still maintained the shop at Greenpoint in Brooklyn, close to his customers.

The pair of goblets (Fig. 23), a wedding gift to Alma and Edward Hauselt ca. 1870, are said to have been made in Brooklyn. The symbolism in the engraving — pheasants and swans for the bride and hunt scenes for the groom — is still rooted in Bohemian tradition, but the style of engraving has the same lightness and delicacy as the Hoare and Dorflinger goblets. This style of engraving can also be seen in an 1874 catalogue of the Boston & Sandwich Glass Company, and its popularity endured until the 1890's.

From 1855 to 1860, there were about 250 glass cutters working in this country, mostly in the East. During and after the Civil War, their number declined sharply, and the Panic of 1873 further reduced the demand for cut glass. In 1865, only eight flint glass firms survived of the forty-odd founded earlier in the century — five in New England and three in the New York City area. Their principal trade was in globes and shades for lamps as well as chandeliers, according to a contemporary source.

Fig. 23.

The Philadelphia Centennial

By the opening of the Philadelphia Centennial in 1876, the relative simplicity of mid-century cut glass was being replaced by more deeply-cut and elaborate designs, precursors of what is today called the "brilliant" style. Dorflinger exhibited a cut decanter and thirty-eight wineglasses (Fig. 24), one for each state. The intricate cutting, a bold use of intersecting straight lines, took great advantage of the brilliance of the glass and the thickness of the blank, and created the glittering effect of a mass of diamonds.

The Centennial exhibit presaged a tremendous revival in the cut glass industry, which was then at its lowest ebb. Dorflinger's White Mills factory, Gillinder in Philadelphia, the New England Glass Company, the Boston & Sandwich Glass Company, the Mt. Washington Glass Company in New

Fig. 24.

Bedford, Massachusetts, the Meriden Flint Glass Works in Connecticut, and the Corning Glass Works were the only manufacturers of blanks for cutting in the country. Cut glass was produced by all of the above-mentioned firms except Corning Glass Works. John Hoare cut blanks supplied by Corning, and there were a few independent cutting shops in New York City. Aside from some minor decorative engraving on cheap tablewares, the fine glass industry was limited in the 1870's to this handful of firms.

Gillinder & Company of Philadelphia operated a complete glass factory on the Centennial grounds, primarily selling pressed souvenir pieces which were very popular. The Gillinder firm also exhibited four engraved pieces of superior quality with birds, foliage, and the familiar running horses of Bohemian tradition (Fig. 25A, B). Unfortunately, Gillinder records do not mention the name of the engraver. The New England firms also exhibited at the Centennial. The cut plate (Fig. 26) in the Boston & Sandwich Glass Company's display was designed and cut by Nehemiah Packwood, head of the cutting shop.

The Boston & Sandwich plate and a cut decanter set exhibited by the New England Glass Company, although not as innovative as the Dorflinger cut set, had some characteristics of the new cut style. The engraved pieces exhibited by Gillinder, Dorflinger, and by the New England Glass Company were old-fashioned by comparison.

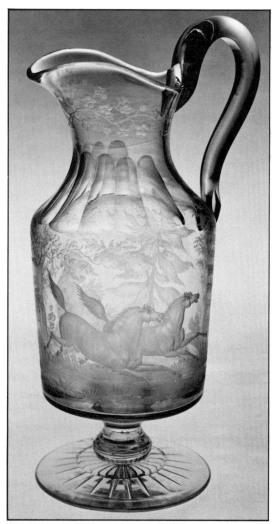

Fig. 25A.

Fig. 25B.

The small wineglass (Fig. 27), inscribed "New England Glass Company Boston" on one side and "Mass. Cent^l Head Q^{rs} 1876" on the reverse, was part of a decanter set exhibited by the New England Glass Company, and it is clearly in the style of the 1860's—a style which would prevail until the 1890's.

Joseph Haselbauer, an engraver from Corning, set up a tent on the Centennial grounds where he engraved glass on his foot-powered lathe. His wife sold his glass.

The Centennial exhibition catalogue shows cut and engraved glasses chiefly in the displays of the Eastern glasshouses. The eleven Pittsburgh glass companies decided to show their wares in one long case; most of it was pressed glass, lighting devices, and containers. The Bakewell Company, perhaps because of its long tradition of glass cutting, did exhibit an enormous cut fruit stand and an engraved punch bowl. There were also several European exhibitors of cut glass, and the Jury singled out the display of the Austrian firm of Lobmeyr for special praise.

The attention these exhibits attracted and the growing United States prosperity led to a new era in the cut glass industry. Orders for cut glass began to come in from the South and West, and although the number of factories supplying blanks did not grow substantially, their production did, while independent cutters and cutting shops proliferated. The demand for cut glass increased every year thereafter until World War I. By 1905, the principal manufacturers were located in White Mills, Pennsylvania, Toledo, Ohio, and Corning, New York. Corning, known as the "Crystal City" by 1900, had a number of highly skilled Bohemian engravers and was unique in having a glassworks and cutting shops independent of each other but bound by family ties which endured for two generations.

Fig. 26.

Fig. 27.

Cutting and Engraving in Corning, New York

The story of the glass industry in Corning is based on an interlocking relationship of individual businessmen, glassmakers, cutters, engravers, and the multitude of companies which marketed their products. The names sometimes become little more than a bewildering list, but these men were the creators of some of the most exquisite glass ever made. Their story begins in Brooklyn in 1864 when the glass works near the South Ferry, formerly occupied by the bankrupt Brooklyn Flint Glass Works, was acquired by the Houghton family of Somerville, Massachusetts. Hoare & Dailey, a Brooklyn cutting firm, owned the company's cutting department. As the Amory Houghtons, Sr. and Jr., strove to make the factory successful, labor troubles and fire conspired against them. Near Corning, meanwhile, Elias Hungerford had patented a glass window blind and was looking for a manufacturer willing to move to Corning. He approached the Houghtons in 1866. Two years passed, but finally Hungerford raised $50,000; the Brooklyn men raised $75,000 and agreed to move. The chief attraction for investors may have been that Hoare & Dailey agreed to open a cutting shop in the new factory, even though their Greenpoint shop continued to operate. In return the Houghtons agreed not to sell cutting blanks to Hoare & Dailey's competitors.

Construction of the new factory began in Corning in the spring of 1868 when Amory Houghton and his brother-in-law, Henry P. Sinclaire, came to town as the new Corning Flint Glass Works president and secretary. Corning residents followed the factory's progress with great interest, and when the plant opened that fall, crowds of curious visitors interfered with production. Corning's love affair with fine glass had begun.

Fig. 28.

Hoare & Dailey, established on the factory's second floor, employed among their craftsmen at least one engraver. The factory made molds for Elias Hungerford's glass blind in 1869 and again in 1871; it sold modestly in the Corning area, but was never really successful. Blanks for Hoare & Dailey's cut glass, on the other hand, were an important glass works product. Although Hoare's firm was always an entirely separate business, the two companies were inextricably interwoven in the mind of the Corning community. Hoare & Dailey was often referred to as "the Glass Works cutting shop."

The period immediately prior to the Civil War had been a prosperous one for cut glass manufacturers, but the War started a decline which persisted through the Depression of 1873-1876. During this period, the Pennsylvania coal which fueled the Corning Flint Glass Works was found to be full of slate, and a major flood in 1870 stopped railroad shipments for several days and canal shipment for weeks. The company shut down its furnaces and went into receivership in 1870. In spite of this, in December Corning citizens read in the *Corning Weekly Journal* that the glass company had received an order for glass for the White House. Hoare & Dailey presumably cut it at their Greenpoint shop.

The glass company reopened in 1871, and in 1872 Amory Houghton, Jr., bought the company on credit. John Hoare showed his confidence in the new organization by clos-

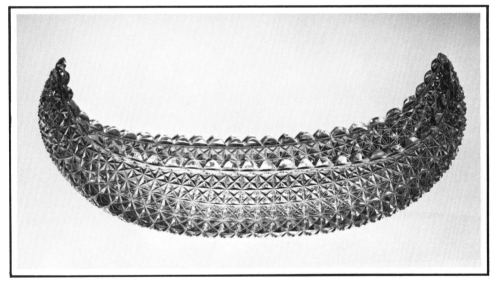

Fig. 29.

ing his Brooklyn shop in 1873 and bringing his workmen to Corning, where he himself bought a house. Another White House order was received that August, and this one was cut in Corning. Local pride was so strong that the ladies of the Episcopal church exhibited the glass for a fee and raised a considerable sum for "good works." As business improved, Amory and Charles Houghton, Henry Sinclaire, and a fourth associate who later sold his interest in the firm, incorporated Corning Glass Works in January 1875.

Business in Corning expanded. In 1880 Thomas G. Hawkes, former manager for Hoare & Dailey, opened his Hawkes Rich Cut Glass Works on Market Street with seven or eight cutters. John Hoare and

Fig. 30.

Corning Glass Works considered Hawkes' company a necessary enlargement of the industry, not a competitor; the Glass Works sold blanks to Hawkes from the company's beginning.

Like the rest of America, the Corning community was vigorous and confident. The sixty-hour work week did not drain the vast reservoir of her citizens' energy. The residents not only supported an astonishing number of fraternal and social organizations but attended a succession of balls, outings, and formal receptions. Business was "the founder of the feast" in Corning as elsewhere. As the population climbed toward 5,000, residents took note of each new design patented. Manufacturers prided themselves on selling what they produced: their representatives traveled so much that newspapers ran train schedules as news items. Politically, Corning glassmen were strong Republicans. It had been clear since the 1840's that American glass could not compete against Europe's low-wage product without protective tariffs, but the opposing Democrats believed in tariffs for revenue only.

The census of 1880 listed thirty-nine cutters in the town of Corning, up from five in 1870. Engravers were two, Augustus and Joseph Haselbauer, working for Hoare and Hawkes respectively. Until the late 1880's, Hoare and Hawkes cuttings were of the straight-line style characteristic of English work (Figs. 28, 29). Neither company used a trade mark. In 1883 H.P. Sinclaire, Jr., son of the Corning Glass Works' secretary, went to work for Hawkes. Sinclaire strongly preferred engraving to cutting and began to design engraved pieces, though few found their way to market.

The slow summer season, when cutters worked "short time" of three or four days a week, was unusually long in 1885. A White House order arrived at the Hawkes company in late September; evidently it was shared with Hoare & Dailey, since both companies returned to full-time work the same day. The fifty dozen pieces were of gold-ruby, amber, and crystal. Their "Russian" cutting, a Hawkes design patented in 1882, "shone with the brilliancy of ten thousand closely-set jewels," the newspaper noted (Fig. 30). Joseph Haselbauer engraved the Presidential emblem. In 1889, President Harrison ordered additional glasses for the White House in the same pattern from C. Dorflinger & Sons in White Mills, Pennsylvania. This set is said to have been sent to Corning for Haselbauer to engrave the Presidential seal (Fig. 31).

The slow season of 1886 ended less fortunately when sixty of Hawkes' 100 employ-

Fig. 31.

ees went on strike. The issues were the right to join a union and the company's inordinate number of apprentices. The strike ended in 1887 with Corning still a resolutely non-union town, a fact which strongly influenced her future. That the workers raised the issue of apprentices emphasizes the popularity of apprentice programs in the days when there were no public high schools. Hawkes had more apprentice applicants, apparently, than his cutters thought acceptable. Hoare also had an apprentice shop with its own foreman.

In 1880, the Glass Works had blown the first light bulb blank for Thomas Edison, and in November, 1886, The Glass Works installed electric lights in its plant. The following year Hoare patented an "Electric Light Radiator" of "Rich Cut Flint Glass," which was a cut glass bulb cover to diffuse the glare of the new lights (Fig. 28). Around this time Hoare sold George L. Abbott, a brother-in-law of Corning Glass Works' Amory Houghton, Jr., a part interest in his firm, which was reorganized as J. Hoare & Co.

In 1888, the problem of competing against Europe was brought into clear focus. The *New York Tribune* listed comparative wages: German cutters earned $3.00 weekly; a good English cutter made $7.00 to $9.00; his American counterpart earned $14.00 to $20.00. H.P. Sinclaire, Jr., speaking for the Hawkes company, noted that European manufacturers regularly copied American patterns and designs. During this period prominent dealers customarily sold American cut glass as "English," and it took a massive advertising campaign by American manufacturers to promote the idea that American cut glass was as good as or better than English.

In the early 1880's, prestigious orders for both cutting and engraving had arrived. A pair of toilet bottles for W.H. Vanderbilt

were engraved in 1881 with "a steamer in full sail, the telegraph, and a railroad scene." Vanderbilt received a $500 punch bowl in 1883 with cutting reminiscent of "dazzling clusters of diamonds" and engravings which included railroad scenes and coke ovens. Both orders were placed with Hawkes and presumably engraved by Joseph Haselbauer. As Haselbauer worked on the Vanderbilt punch bowl, Thomas Webb's blowers in England were fashioning the blank for a piece of glass that would

Fig. 33.

change Corning's glassmaking history. That piece, the Fritsche ewer, was completed in 1886 after two and a half years of engraving. Its high relief polished engraving, a style that Webb called "rock crystal," was the work of Master engraver William Fritsche of Meistersdorf, Bohemia (Fig. 32). A specialty of Bohemians, "rock crystal" required deep carving of a large portion of the blank, which was then finished by copper-wheel engraving. The three-dimensional result differed sharply

Fig. 32.

from Corning's two-dimensional pictorial engravings, exemplified by the pair of cologne bottles made around 1890 in the Hoare or Hawkes shop (Fig. 33).

In the Continental system, a Master engraver had completed seven or more years of training. His designation as Master engraver conferred the privileges of teaching and of operating his own shop. The candidate had to be recommended as a man of dignity and high moral standards. Such a man was William Fritsche, and such a man, too, was Corning's Joseph Haselbauer.

Theodore Starr, a New York jeweler, bought the Fritsche ewer, and the ensuing publicity described Fritsche as "as true an artist as ever breathed." It is unlikely that cutting enthusiasts John Hoare and Thomas Hawkes had ever considered the distinction between high skill and art before, but they had reason to be sensitive to the successes of English glassmakers.

Thomas Hawkes reacted almost at once. Probably he had already decided to exhibit at the Paris Universal Exposition of 1889; now he agreed to include engraved pieces, which H.P. Sinclaire designed and Joseph Haselbauer engraved (Fig. 34). As Haselbauer worked on the Paris glass, another Meistersdorf engraver reached Corning and went to work for Hawkes. He appeared in Corning directories as William Fritchie for several years. Later he changed the listing to "Hieronimus William Fritchie."

The Hawkes company sent 612 pieces of glass to the Paris Exposition. Except for two Dorflinger-made punch bowls, all the blanks were from Corning Glass Works; the exhibit won a gold medal. Corning celebrated the news with a brass band and torchlight parade. Charles Houghton, Amory's brother, and John Hoare made speeches, and the Corning *Journal* wrote that the prize will "doubtless lead to largely in-

Fig. 34.

creased orders," which it did. Unfortunately, few pieces are left from that exhibit.

Hawkes' Paris success prompted him to reorganize his company and adopt a trademark, printed on a paper sticker until 1899 and acid-stamped thereafter. The new name was T.G. Hawkes & Co. Manager Oliver Egginton received a share of stock and the title of partner; H.P. Sinclaire, Jr., bought twelve and a half percent of the stock. By raising Sinclaire's salary to the level of his own, Hawkes effectively endorsed Sinclaire's plan to make the company name synonymous with fine engraving.

Another Meistersdorf glass carver, Fridoli Kretschmann, was in Corning by 1891, presumably to work on J. Hoare & Co.'s

exhibit for the 1893 Columbian Exposition in Chicago. Judges admired Hoare cuttings as well as engravings and awarded four medals to the company for glassware, "rock crystal" cutting, cut glass, and engraved glass. Hoare's chef-d'oeuvre for this exhibition was a massive twenty-four inch punch bowl which has since disappeared. Hoare adopted an acid-stamped trademark shortly after the exhibit.

Joseph Nitsche and Adolf Kretschmann of Meistersdorf left Webb in Stourbridge, came to Corning, and went to work as engravers for T.G. Hawkes & Co. in 1893. Hawkes and Hoare considered themselves colleagues in the struggle to establish Corning as the leading center of fine-glass production. They worked together on large orders, and they did not compete against

Fig. 35.

Fig. 36.

each other at world's fairs. The decanter (Fig. 35) is an example of Hoare's later "rock crystal" style; the bowl (Fig. 36) is from T.G. Hawkes.

The acid dip, which made it possible to eliminate the hand-polishing of glass, was an innovation of the 1890's. Hawkes and Hoare continued to hand-polish after the acid dip, but by 1900, they, too, were offering a less expensive line of glass as well as their top-quality products. At about the same time, they began to buy blanks from sources other than Corning Glass Works: a few from Union Glass Works, Pairpoint, H.C. Fry, Libbey, Webb in England, Baccarat in France, Val St. Lambert in Belgium, and many from Dorflinger. When the decade ended, Hawkes was buying more blanks from Dorflinger than from Corning Glass Works. His Dorflinger blanks were chiefly tablewares; the Glass Works continued to make blanks for his heaviest vases, bowls, and pitchers. Cutters in Corning had increased from 185 to 360, engravers from four to nine.

About 1886, John S. O'Connor had introduced the curved miter cut which made possible the exuberant decoration which

Fig. 37.

Fig. 38.

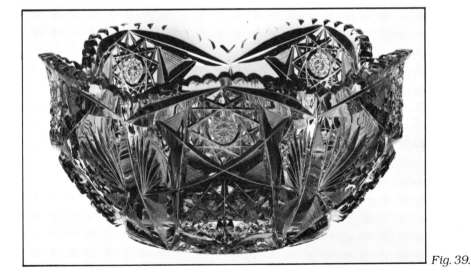

Fig. 39.

45

flourished at the turn of the century. Examples are the Hoare bowls (Figs. 37-39) and punch bowl (Fig. 40). Examples from Hawkes are a large plate in the "Russian" pattern, cut around 1906 (Fig. 41), the "Queen's" pattern lamp (Fig. 42), and the plate (Fig. 43). The square bowl (Fig. 44) was a wedding present to a Corning couple in 1909. The tray (Fig. 45), cut in an unusual pattern of interlocking circles, and the simply-cut urn (Fig. 46), one of a pair, are departures from Hawkes' usual "brilliant" cutting.

Two additional cutting companies opened in the 1890's—Hunt & Sullivan (1895) and the O.F. Egginton Co. (1896). They used virtually no Corning or Dorflinger blanks. Thomas Hunt and Oliver Egginton, both Englishmen, were former Hawkes employees. Hunt's company, with financial backing from Daniel Sullivan, prospered, at first doing mainly standard cut patterns. "Royal," patented in 1911, was their most popular pattern for twenty years (Fig. 47). The large jug (Fig. 48), a special order around 1915, was cut on a Pairpoint blank by Lee

Fig. 40.

Fig. 41.

Fig. 42.

Fig. 43.

Fig. 44.

Fig. 45.

Fig. 46.

Fig. 47.

Fig. 48.

Carr and engraved by Joseph Libisch in his home shop. Walter Egginton, Oliver's son, was the Egginton designer; he had designed for Hawkes. His "Trellis" pattern (Fig. 49) is especially fine. The "Strathmore" compote and "Virginia" lamp are also Egginton pieces (Figs. 50, 51).

Steuben Glass Works, managed by Frederick Carder and financed by T.G. Hawkes, opened in 1903, followed by H.P. Sinclaire & Co. in 1904. Both were noted for the fine quality of their cut and engraved products. Most of Hawkes' engraving department, including Joseph Haselbauer, followed Sinclaire when he left Hawkes to start his own firm. His chief suppliers of blanks were Dorflinger and Corning Glass Works. Hawkes began to use Steuben blanks and stopped buying from Dorflinger, as did Hoare.

Frederick Carder's "Aurene" and other colored glasses made Steuben famous. Carder disliked cut glass, but he produced it from the beginning. The "brilliant" cut plate (Fig. 52) and "rock crystal" ewer (Fig. 53) are similar in style to the products of other companies, but the colored glass made in the 1920's (Figs. 54-57) and the plain cut and engraved glass of the Thirties (Fig. 58) are perhaps better known.

H.P. Sinclaire & Co. made some "brilliant"

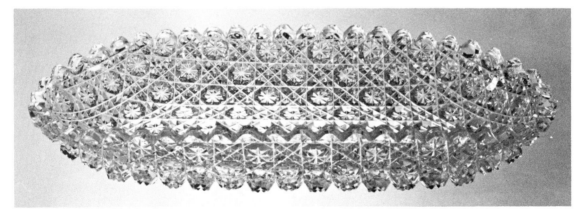

Fig. 49.

cut glass (Fig. 59), but its founder was most interested in engraving—both "rock crystal" style (Figs. 60, 61, 62) and figural. The decanter (Fig. 60) and cologne, like the tall vase (Fig. 34), were designed by H.P. Sinclaire for the Hawkes entry in the Paris Exposition of 1889. All three designs were produced later by Sinclaire's own firm.

Fig. 50.

Fig. 51.

From 1894 through 1910, a number of smaller short-lived companies opened as well as firms which were only subcontractors. Frank Wilson & Sons, in 1894, was the first of these. Wilson was an English cutter, and some of his glass was cut in the English style (Fig. 63). His factory was closed by 1897. Others of short duration were the Knockerbocker Cut Glass Company, 1902; Almy & Thomas, 1903-1907 (Fig. 64); the George W. Drake Cut Glass Company, ca. 1899-1908; the Corning Cut Glass Company, ca. 1901-1911; Painter glass cutting shop, ca. 1904-1905 (Fig. 65); the Standard Cut Glass Company, 1905-1908 (Fig. 66). Giometti Brothers, on the

Fig. 53.

Fig. 52.

53

Fig. 54.

Fig. 55.

Fig. 56.

Fig. 57.

Fig. 58.

Fig. 60.

Fig. 59.

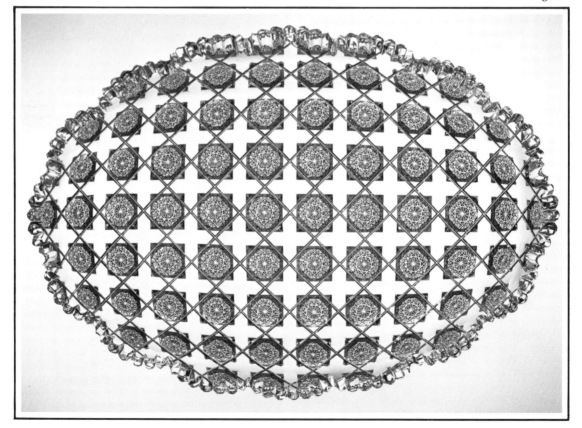

Fig. 61.

Fig. 62.

Fig. 63.

Fig. 64.

Fig. 65.

Fig. 66.

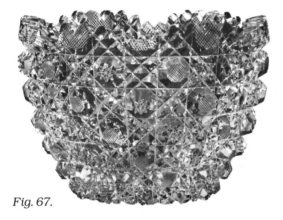

Fig. 67.

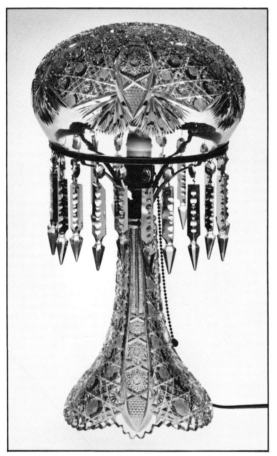

Fig. 68.

other hand, operated from 1902 to 1933. It was headed by Clarence Giometti, who had probably trained as a cutter at Hawkes (Figs. 67, 68).

Corning's glassmakers were proud of Corning's reputation. "Corning cut glass," they believed, meant quality to the jewelers to whom they sold. Consequently, Corning Glass Works sued the principals of Corning Cut Glass Company over the use of the name. Testimony during the suit in 1904 and 1906 gives much information on the state of the industry. Thomas Hawkes testified that he paid a premium for Corning Glass Works blanks because their high lead content kept them from changing color during the acid dip. Corning blanks, however, were available only to Hawkes, Hoare, and Sinclaire. Why, then, did so many other cutting firms open in Corning? The president of Corning Cut Glass gave his reasons. They were: Corning's reputation for fine glass, its supply of skilled craftsmen, and finally, its lack of unionization. Undoubtedly, the second and third reasons were important to the branch cutting shops of out-of-town companies that quietly opened in Corning. Branches of Elmira Cut Glass and Eygabroat-Ryon were both located at 63 Erie Avenue in Corning. The Majestic Cut Glass Co. (Fig. 69), whose Corning shop location is unknown, used Belgian blanks, probably from Val St. Lambert, and was an Elmira-based operation. Eygabroat-Ryon was a Lawrenceville, Pennsylvania, firm whose foreman, Everett Stage, was trained at Hawkes around the turn of the century. He later started his own cutting shop, Stage-Kashins, in Lawrenceville. He cut the compote (Fig. 70) at one of the two Lawrenceville shops.

Corning's influence spread far beyond its borders as men trained at Hawkes and Hoare moved elsewhere. Charles Rose of Ideal Cut Glass moved his company from Corning to Canastota, New York, in 1905, where it flourished until 1933. The punch bowl (Fig. 71) was cut there in 1912-1915. Charles Tuthill, son of Corning's most important architect, was trained at Hawkes. He and his brother James started the Tuthill Glass Company in Middletown, New York, around 1900. Tuthill was never a large firm, but the quality of its glass made it nationally famous. The lamp in the "Rex"

Fig. 69.

Fig. 70.

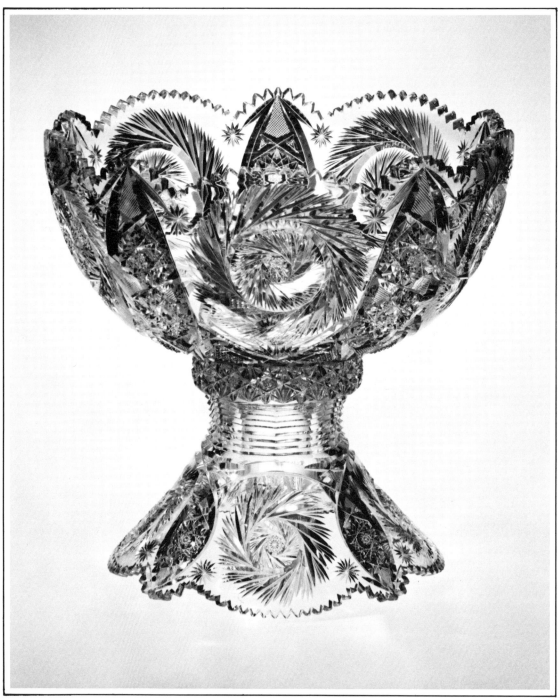

Fig. 71.

Fig. 72.

Fig. 73.

pattern (Fig. 72) and the "Vintage" punch set (Fig. 73) are typical of Tuthill products. The small bowl (Fig. 74) was cut and stone-engraved by Leon Swope at Tuthill around 1912-1913. In his fourteen year career, he worked for seven firms from coast to coast.

In 1905, there were 490 cutters in Corning and thirty-three engravers. By 1909, the number of cutters had decreased to 340. As cut glass quality dropped, the industry's center shifted to the New York City area, where cutting firms were willing to cheapen their products in order to sell to department stores.

Hunt, Egginton, and Steuben followed the Bohemian practice of subcontracting their engraving. This was done by Joseph Hasel-

Fig. 74.

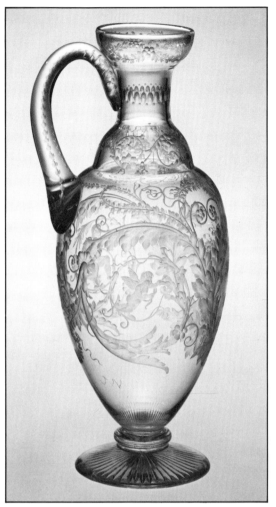

Fig. 75.

Fig. 76.

bauer and his son Fred; Joseph Nitsche (Fig. 75) and his son Clement (Fig. 76); and H.W. Fritchie. All were designers as well as engravers. Around 1900, Fritchie and Haselbauer trained Corning's first American-born engravers, Wilmot Putnam (Fig. 77), William Morse, and Hiram Rouse, all of whom began at Hawkes working on the new "Gravic" line of unpolished engravings. The design of the Fritchie pitcher with portraits of President and Mrs. McKinley (Fig. 78), engraved around 1901, is similar in design to Hiram Rouse's self-portrait engraved on a pitcher about 1905 (Fig. 79). The Haselbauer family built a small, well-equipped factory behind their house about 1910, but Joseph died before it opened in 1911. The firm, J.F. Haselbauer & Sons, advertised "Rich Rock Crystal, Copper-Wheel and Stone Engraving." Frederick S. Haselbauer and his younger brother George M. operated the shop until 1920 when George left. Frederick engraved there alone until 1938. The pair of vases were engraved by Frederick and George Haselbauer for their mother (Fig. 80). The single vase (Fig. 81) is the work of George.

By 1905, Corning's Bohemian engravers included Anthony and Henry Keller, the Hauptmanns, and Ernest Kaulfuss (Fig. 82), all from Meistersdorf, and Master engraver Edward Palme (Fig. 83) from another village. A talented successor to Joseph Haselbauer arrived in Corning in April of 1911. Master engraver Joseph Libisch, who worked for both Sinclaire and Steu-

Fig. 77.

Fig. 78.

Fig. 79.

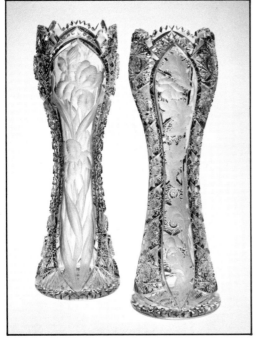

Fig. 80.

Fig. 81.

Fig. 82.

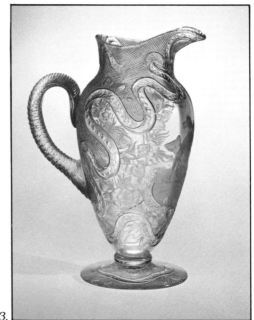

Fig. 83.

Fig. 84.

Fig. 85.

ben, was the link between Corning's past and her glassmaking future (Figs. 84, 85).

John Illig was an Alsatian engraver who won a prize at the Paris Exposition of 1899. He came to Corning in 1902 and went to work first for Hawkes and then for Sinclaire. The tray in Figure 86 is a Sinclaire piece which was probably engraved by Illig. The small vase (Fig. 87) was engraved in 1905 on a broken Sinclaire blank. Its design is obviously influenced by Illig's European background and training. Illig started his own shop on Tioga Avenue in 1915, and in 1921 he moved into the vacant Egginton factory where he operated until about 1929. He continued to engrave designs (Fig. 88) that had been his specialty at the Sinclaire company.

Corning's glass factories were the city's preferred employers. Young women coveted jobs they offered, and schoolgirls were eager to "help out" during busy periods. Women could become supervisors or chief inspectors; the Hunt Glass Co.'s business manager was a woman. Girls also enjoyed washing and polishing the glass, which they said looked like "a mass of diamonds." Larger glass companies continued to work together. Many sets of tablewares are trademarked by two or more of them. The goblets (Fig. 89) bear the trademarks of Hoare and Sinclaire respectively; the smaller wines are not marked.

The "figured blank," which came into use about 1910, had the chief elements of cut designs pressed into it. Figured blanks, which were not much used in Corning, were important in cost cutting, but they brought about a monotony of design that alienated discerning buyers. Polished engravings, which could not be mechanically pressed, became increasingly popular. Stone engravings, which now included much Hawkes "Gravic" glass, were less expensive than "rock crystal" and often

Fig. 86.

Fig. 87.

Fig. 88.

Fig. 89.

most attractive (Fig. 90). "Gang wheels," which made several parallel cuts at a time, date from about 1913 (Fig. 88).

Peter A. Eick, a Hawkes cutter, opened a cutting shop behind his house in 1912 and operated it until 1935, selling his products locally year round and out-of-town at Christmas time. His wife and daughter washed and packed his glass. Such one-man shops enabled cutters to make ends meet during the all-too-frequent layoffs by major firms. Almost every cutter and engraver in Corning had a cutting wheel or a lathe in his basement or shed. Adolf Kretschmann was an engraver like Eick who had private customers (Fig. 91), but few sold their glass as widely as Eick.

As World War I began, shipments of Bac-

Fig. 90.

Fig. 91.

Fig. 92.

carat and Val St. Lambert blanks to the United States ceased. C. Dorflinger & Sons stopped making crystal. In 1918, Corning Glass Works bought Steuben Glass Works from Hawkes and used the factory to increase production of light bulbs. Thus, only a trickle of fine glass continued. The gloom failed to prevent Mrs. Fred (Nell) Fuller, who had long been business manager of Hunt Glass Company, from opening a small cutting shop about 1916. Glass that can be confidently attributed to her firm is intaglio cut (Fig. 92).

During a depression that began in 1920, J. Hoare & Co. closed. The company was then being managed by the third generation of Hoares cutting glass in Corning. When the depression ended in 1922, a craze for colored glass had begun, and European imports rose sharply. Corning met the first challenge; a flood of colored glass poured from H.P. Sinclaire's small blowing factory and Steuben's large one to be etched, hand-painted, and even sold undecorated (Figs. 54, 55, 93, 94, 95). Intaglio cuttings increasingly imitated the more expensive engraved wares. High quality cutting and engraving continued, but there were fewer orders. Joseph Libisch stopped working in the Sinclaire factory to devote full time to subcontracting from his home shop. As the years passed, his work for Steuben took more and more of his time, and it was he who distributed Steuben's engraving to Corning's other shops.

During Prohibition, wine and cocktail glasses were still being made in Corning, as documented in Corning catalogues. Obviously, those who could afford fine glass were still drinking. The trouble was, as rising import figures show, that more and more people were using European glasses.

The final battle of the war of costs began in the 1920's. Cheap fuel could not close the gap between high American wages and

Fig. 93.

Fig. 94.

those in Europe. The Great Depression made matters worse. What, then, were the options? H.P. Sinclaire reasoned that he must subsidize his fine glass by making commercial specialties such as baking ware, and he built a factory in which to do so. His death in 1927 changed those plans, and the Sinclaire factory closed in 1928. The Hawkes company elected to add less expensive lines; enameled glass and increased quantities of gold-rimmed tablewares were among them. Hunt gradually phased out its "rock crystal" engravings and its "Waterford" cuttings, turning instead to intaglio cutting. Figures 96 and 97 illustrate the simpler designs that Hunt began to make in the late 1930's. By this time, the company was using pressed and figured blanks as well as blown. Hunt continued to pioneer; the number of women cutters increased until they outnumbered the men.

Fig. 95.

Fig. 96.

Fig. 97.

Fig. 98.

Corning received another White House cut glass order in 1938 when Franklin Roosevelt ordered a new set of glass from T.G. Hawkes & Co. Roosevelt at first intended to order replacements for the "Russian" set supplied by Hawkes in 1885 and Dorflinger in 1889, but on learning the price, he chose a simpler design (Fig. 98). Hawkes was still selling "Gravic" engraved glass and had added a number of simple cut patterns (Fig. 99 A, B, C) to his more elaborate designs.

Meanwhile, Corning Glass Works considered a new path. Its Steuben Division was unprofitable, and there was every reason

Fig. 99A.   Fig. 99B.   Fig. 99C.

to close it. Yet in 1933 the Glass Works' directors agreed to a change that would have been possible nowhere else. Arthur A. Houghton, Jr., proposed a goal of great simplicity—the manufacture of the finest crystal in the world. He envisioned using a newly-developed glass so pure that it required no decolorizer. The glass itself would be a new medium for artists; they would

Fig. 100.

design art objects rather than utilitarian pieces to which decoration was added. The production and sale of cutting blanks would stop.

John Monteith Gates, an architect, was hired as Steuben's Director of Design; he and sculptor Sidney Waugh designed all Steuben glass made for the first three years. The first major engraved design, Waugh's Gazelle Bowl, engraved by Joseph Libisch in 1935 (Fig. 100), was among the pieces shown in major exhibits in London and New York. These exhibits established the company as an innovator in glass design. Steuben Glass won awards at the World's Fairs of 1937, 1939, and 1940.

The first Steuben exhibit of designs by contemporary artists opened in 1940. Again, a concept new to glass was based firmly on the matchless skill of Corning's engravers. Four of them were now working in the Steuben factory. Joseph Libisch, foreman, and Clement Nitsche were teaching Steuben's first apprentice engravers.

Steuben's success renewed Corning's faith in her future as a fine-glass center. Today there are quality repair shops, home engraving shops, and cutters who fashion jewelry from old art glass and crystal. A new five-frame company specializes in intaglio cutting, and courses in engraving are offered at Corning Community College.

The new beginning is apposite to that of 1868. Orders from the White House and medals at world's fairs proved to John Hoare and Thomas Hawkes that their glass was the finest in the world. When England challenged American supremacy, H.P. Sinclaire assembled an unsurpassed group of engravers in Corning. Only their skills made Steuben's new conceptions a reality. A new beginning, yes, but also a fresh chapter of a story that began in 1868. Its end is not in sight.

Colleagues and Competitors

Corning, of course, was not the only town in which cut glass played a major role at the turn of the century. C. Dorflinger & Sons of White Mills, Pennsylvania, and the Libbey Glass Company in Toledo, Ohio, were its major competitors. It is important to realize that all of these firms cooperated in the manufacture and distribution of blanks, and workmen were sometimes loaned by one company to another. It was rare for anyone to spend his entire working career in one factory. This is one of the reasons why it is difficult to identify unmarked cut glass. Cutting shops opened all over the country, literally from coast to coast, but most of the important firms, in terms of both quantity and quality, are represented in this last section of the catalogue.

C. Dorflinger & Sons of White Mills was one of the oldest companies, having been started in Brooklyn in the mid-nineteenth century (see Figs. 13, 18, 21, 22, 24, 31). In 1881, Christian Dorflinger incorporated as C. Dorflinger & Sons, a name which lasted until 1921 when the firm closed. The cutting shop in White Mills was opened in 1867. Dorflinger was both a large supplier of fine quality blanks and a cutting shop whose name became synonymous with quality wares. The kerosene lamp (Fig. 101) and the large, probably unique vase (Fig. 102) both date from the 1880's. The latter was formerly in the collection of Louis Dorflinger, Christian's son. The restrained geometric style of both of these pieces is typical of the 1880's before "pinwheels" and "hobstars" became the vogue. The green punch set (Fig. 103) in the "Montrose" pattern is a design of the 1890's. Four of these bowls, all cased in green, are known. The wineglass (Fig. 104) probably dates from after 1890. Its swirled design is similar to that found on many "rock crystal" engraved pieces. The ruby-

Fig. 101.

Fig. 102.

Fig. 103.

Fig. 104.

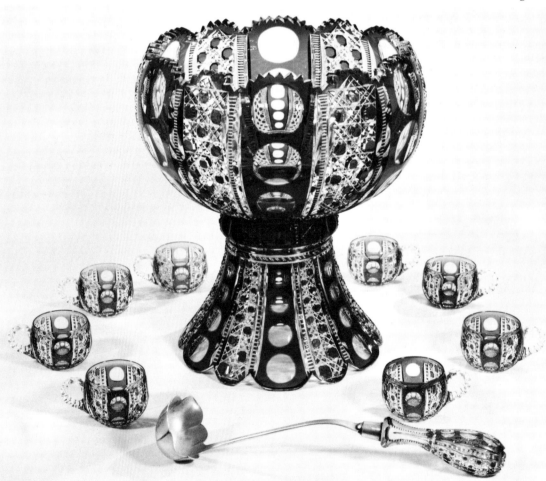

cased glasses (Fig. 105) are like those in a set ordered by the Prince of Wales when he toured the United States and Canada in 1918-1919.

The other early significant center for glass cutting in the United States was Toledo, Ohio, home of the Libbey Glass Company, founded by Edward D. Libbey after the closing of his New England Glass Company of Cambridge, Massachusetts. Libbey moved the company to Ohio in 1888. Libbey, like Hawkes and Dorflinger, advertised its cut glass in major women's magazines and it was probably the largest single firm manufacturing cut glass in the United States. The company was also a major supplier of cutting blanks, though it sold few to Corning's large firms.

Imitating Gillinder's techniques at the Centennial, Libbey erected a glasshouse on the grounds of the World's Colombian Exposition in Chicago in 1893. Adolf Kretschmann demonstrated cutting for Libbey at the fair before coming to Corning. The engraved punch set and the cut lamp (Figs. 106, 107) were both part of Libbey's exhibit at that fair.

Libbey's display at the Louisiana Purchase Exposition in St. Louis in 1904 included the large plate, "Apotheosis of Transportation" (Fig. 109), which is a tour de force of engraving, an engraved table service, a mammoth twenty-five inch punch bowl, and a thirty inch cut table. The "Transportation" plate and several other pieces, including two engraved plaques (Figs. 110, 111) that illustrate glass cutting and engraving, were presented to the Smithsonian Institution by Libbey in 1905 as part of a comprehensive exhibit on the cut glass industry.

The large cut punch bowl is a twin to one made for presentation to President William McKinley in 1898 (Fig. 108). The original has disappeared, unfortunately, and this

Fig. 105.

Fig. 106.

Fig. 107.

Fig. 109.

Fig. 110.

Fig. 111.

back-up piece was sold by Libbey in 1905. Glasshouses ordinarily made two exhibition and presentation pieces so that if anything happened to one, time would not be lost in replacing it. Another large supplier of blanks was the Pairpoint Manufacturing Company of New Bedford, Massachusetts.

H.C. Fry Glass Company of Rochester, Pennsylvania, organized in 1901, also supplied blanks to firms in the Corning area. Perhaps inspired by Libbey's successful exhibition of the table and mammoth punch bowl in 1904, the Fry Company produced a four and one half foot tall punch bowl ensemble (Fig. 112), which won a Grand Medal of Honor at the Lewis and Clark Exposition at Portland, Oregon, in 1905.

An immense candelabrum was bought by Milton Hershey, the chocolate magnate, at the Columbian Exposition in Chicago. It is not possible to determine the manufacturer, but since L. Straus & Sons of New York City received a prize for the larg-

Fig. 112

Fig. 108.

est piece of cut glass shown at the fair, a twelve-foot candelabrum, it seems likely that this is the same piece.

In comparing the exhibition pieces which were shown at the 1893 and 1904 fairs, little stylistic change can be seen. In Corning, 1900 to about 1908 was the time of greatest prosperity for glass cutting firms. As we have seen, cheaper wares, either pressed or cut on figured blanks eventually lessened the appeal of fine cut glass to discerning buyers. Rising wages, the gradual unionization of workmen, and World War I weakened the industry. During the war, raw materials and blanks could not be obtained from Europe, workmen were lost to the war effort, and fuel was scarce for non-essential manufactories. After the war, the severe depression of 1920-1922 shook the glass industry.

J. Hoare & Co. of Corning, the oldest cutting shop in the country, closed its doors in 1920. C. Dorflinger & Sons closed permanently in 1921. By the late Thirties, T.G. Hawkes & Co., Hunt Glass Works, and Steuben Glass, all in Corning, and Libbey in Toledo were the only major cutting firms still operating in the United States, and all were making other lines of glass as well. Pieces of cut and engraved glass like those in this exhibition were no longer in demand. Although it is no longer economically feasible to make "brilliant" cut glass in the United States, some of the finest glass in the world today is made and engraved in Corning, New York, and turn-of-the-century Corning cut and engraved glass is avidly sought by collectors—the wheel has come full circle.

Catalogue

ANGLO-IRISH AND MIDWESTERN GLASS

1. *Cut decanter.* Anglo-Irish, ca. 1800; H. 21.2 cm, The Corning Museum of Glass (50.2.29A). [Fig. 1]

2. *Cut vase.* Anglo-Irish, ca. 1800; H. 17 cm, The Corning Museum of Glass (50.2.105). [Fig. 2]

3. *Cut decanter.* Bakewell, Page & Bakewell, ca. 1825-1835; H. 27.3 cm, The Corning Museum of Glass (67.4.8). [Fig. 3]

4. *Cut and engraved tumbler* enclosing a sulphide portrait of Washington. Bakewell, Page & Bakewell, ca. 1825; H. 8.5 cm, The Corning Museum of Glass (55.4.57). [Fig. 4]

5. *Cut decanter.* John Robinson & Co., ca. 1835-1845; H. 19.9 cm, Coll: Historical Society of Western Pennsylvania, Pittsburgh, Pennsylvania. Gift of Mrs. J.B. Sellers. (Corning only)

6. *Cut decanter.* R.B. Curling & Sons, 1828; H. 26.7 cm, Coll: The Carnegie Museum of Art, Pittsburgh, Pennsylvania, Gift of Mrs. Edward Albree (46.1.1). [Fig. 5]

7. *Engraved sugar bowl.* Pittsburgh area, ca. 1825-1835; H. 18.3 cm. The Corning Museum of Glass (55.4.51). [Fig. 6]

8. *Cut decanter.* John and Craig Ritchie, ca. 1829-1837; H. 24.9 cm, Coll: Mansion Museum, Oglebay Institute, Wheeling, West Virginia, Gift of Charlotte Crothers Claypool (69.5). [Fig. 7]

9. *Cut celery.* Michael and Thomas Sweeney, ca. 1840 H. 25.8 cm, Coll: Mansion Museum, Oglebay Institute, Wheeling, West Virginia, Gift of Robert W. Ewing (72.254A). [Fig. 8]

10. *Cut salt.* Michael and Thomas Sweeney, ca. 1840; H. 11.5 cm, Coll: Mansion Museum, Oglebay Institute, Wheeling, West Virginia, Gift of Letitia Sweeney Ewing (37.151). [Fig. 9]

NEW ENGLAND

11. *Cut and engraved decanter.* New England Glass Company, ca. 1840-1850; H. 23.3 cm. The Corning Museum of Glass, Gift of Marion Pike (73.4.22). [Fig. 10]

12. *Ruby cased pitcher.* New England Glass Company, engraved by Henry B. Leighton, ca. 1860; H. 17 cm, The Corning Museum of Glass, Gift of Marion Pike (73.4.28). [Fig. 11]

13. *Ruby cased goblet.* New England Glass Company, designed and engraved by Louis Vaupel, ca. 1865-1870; H. 22.8 cm, Coll: The Toledo Museum of Art, Toledo, Ohio, Gift of Edward Drummond Libbey (74.52). [Fig. 12]

14. *Cut compote.* New England Glass Company, ca. 1872-1876; H. 19.2 cm, Coll: The Toledo Museum of Art, Toledo, Ohio (59.25). [Fig. 14]

15. *Ruby cased over white lamp.* Boston & Sandwich Glass Company, ca. 1850; H. 48.3 cm, Coll: The Metropolitan Museum of Art, New York City, Funds from various donors, 1967 (67.7.23). [Fig. 16]

16. *Ruby cased decanter.* Boston & Sandwich Glass Company, engraved by G.T. Lapham, 1867; H. 25.7 cm, Coll: The Metropolitan Museum of Art, New York City, Funds from various donors, 1967 (67.7.22). [Fig. 15]

17. *Engraved compote.* Boston & Sandwich Glass Company, ca. 1867; H. 17.8 cm, Ex. Coll: The Metropolitan Museum of Art, The Corning Museum of Glass (72.4.117). [Fig. 13 right]

PHILADELPHIA-NEW JERSEY

18. *Cut decanter.* Union Flint Glass Company, ca. 1830's; H. 28.4 cm, The Corning Museum of Glass (71.4.82B). [Fig. 17 right]

19. *Cut lamp.* Probably Union Flint Glass Company, ca. 1830's; H. 33.9 cm, The Corning Museum of Glass, Gift of Louise S. Esterly (61.4.97). [Fig. 18]

20. *Cut bowl.* George Dummer & Co., ca. 1830's; L. 27.1 cm, The Corning Museum of Glass (71.4.112). [Fig. 19]

21. *Pale green cut decanter set.* George Dummer & Co. or Brooklyn Flint Glass Company or New York Glass Works, ca. 1835-1845; H. (decanter) 27 cm, Coll: The Metropolitan Museum of Art, New York City, Gift of Berry B. Tracy, 1972 (1972.266.1-7). [Fig. 20]

NEW YORK CITY AREA

22. *Cut compote.* Long Island Flint Glass Works of Christian Dorflinger, ca. 1856; D. 22 cm, The Corning Museum of Glass, Gift of Kathryn Dorflinger Manchee (71.4.130). [Fig. 17 left]

23. *Ewer.* Probably Long Island Flint Glass Works of Christian Dorflinger, ca. 1852-1863; H. 30.8 cm, The Corning Museum of Glass (58.4.1). [Fig. 17 center]

24. *Cut and engraved compote,* from the set ordered by Mary Todd Lincoln for the White House. Glass Works of Christian Dorflinger at Greenpoint, 1861; H. 22.6 cm, Coll: The Metropolitan Museum of Art, New York City, Gift of Kathryn Hait Dorflinger Manchee, 1972 (1972.232.1). [Fig. 21]

25. *Cut and engraved punch cup,* from the set ordered by Mary Todd Lincoln for the White House. Glass Works of Christian Dorflinger at Greenpoint, 1861; H. 10.1 cm, Coll: June Dorflinger Hardy, on loan to The Corning Museum of Glass (L. 41.4.51). [Fig. 22]

26. *Engraved wineglass.* Wayne County Glass Works of Christian Dorflinger, White Mills, Pennsylvania, 1869; H. 15.1 cm, The Corning Museum of Glass, Gift of Kathryn Dorflinger Manchee (71.4.122). [Fig. 13 center]

27. *Engraved goblet.* Hoare & Dailey, 1869; H. 14 cm, The Corning Museum of Glass, Gift of Mrs. P.M. Chamberlain (65.4.15). [Fig. 13 left]

28. *Engraved pair of goblets.* Brooklyn, probably Dobleman & Bailey, Greenpoint, ca. 1870; H. 14.6 cm, 14.8 cm, The Corning Museum of Glass (74.4.102A, B). [Fig. 23]

CENTENNIAL EXHIBIT

29. *Cut and engraved decanter and four wineglasses* representing Connecticut, Maryland, Massachusetts, and Virginia. Part of a set cut and engraved at the Wayne County Glass Works of Christian Dorflinger for exhibition at the Philadelphia Centennial, 1876; H. (decanter) 30.2 cm, Coll: Philadelphia Museum of Art, Philadelphia, Pennsylvania. (76-1693). [Fig. 24]

30. *Engraved pitcher and goblet.* Gillinder & Sons, 1876; H. (pitcher) 23.8 cm, Coll: Philadelphia Museum of Art, Philadelphia, Pennsylvania (06-253, 254). [Fig. 25a and b]

31. *Cut plate.* Boston & Sandwich Glass Company, cut by Nehemiah Packwood, 1876; D. 25.7 cm, Coll: Mr. and Mrs. Jay Doros. [Fig. 26]

32. *Engraved wineglass.* New England Glass Company, 1876; H. 11.3 cm, The Corning Museum of Glass (55.4.64). [Fig. 27]

J. HOARE & CO., 1868-1920

33. *Pair of engraved cologne bottles.* J. Hoare & Co., or T.G. Hawkes & Co., ca. 1890; H. 18.1 cm, The Corning Museum of Glass (55.4.62 A, B). [Fig. 33]

34. *Cut light radiator.* J. Hoare & Co., ca. 1887; L. 15.6 cm, The Corning Museum of Glass (64.4.46). [Fig. 28]

35. *Cut bowl.* J. Hoare & Co., cut by Andrew Callahan, 1893; L. 35.5 cm, Coll: Miss Frances Barrett. (Corning only)

36. *Decanter, engraved in "rock crystal" style.* J. Hoare & Co., ca. 1900-1915; H. 28.3 cm, Coll: Mrs. John S. Hoare. [Fig. 35]

37. *Cut canoe.* J. Hoare & Co., ca. 1890-1900; L. 31.8 cm, The Corning Museum of Glass, Gift of Mrs. P.M. Chamberlain (65.4.23). [Fig. 29]

38. *Cut bowl.* J. Hoare & Co., ca. 1900-1915; D. 20.3 cm, The Corning Museum of Glass, Gift of R. Lee Waterman (76.4.49). [Fig. 37]

39. *Cut bowl.* J. Hoare & Co., ca. 1900-1915; D. 20.7 cm, The Corning Museum of Glass (65.4.27). [Fig. 38]

40. *Cut bowl.* J. Hoare & Co., ca. 1900-1915; D. 21.6 cm, Coll: Robert F. Rockwell III. [Fig. 39]

41. *Two engraved goblets and two engraved wines* from a set part of which is signed by J. Hoare & Co., and part by H.P. Sinclaire & Co., ca. 1904-1915; H. (tallest) 14.7 cm, Coll: Mrs. Estelle Sinclaire Farrar. [Fig. 89]

42. *Cut punch bowl.* J. Hoare & Co., ca. 1915; D. 53.5 cm, The Corning Museum of Glass, Gift of Mr. and Mrs. M.T. Allen (74.4.142). [Fig. 40]

T.G. HAWKES & CO., 1880-1962

43. *Goblet.* Cut in T.G. Hawkes "Russian" pattern, engraved by Joseph Haselbauer, ordered from C. Dorflinger & Sons by President Harrison, 1889; H. 16.2 cm, Coll: June Dorflinger Hardy, on loan to The Corning Museum of Glass (L. 42.4.51). [Fig. 31]

44. *Plate, cut in "Chrysanthemum" pattern,* exhibited at the Paris Exposition of 1889. Hawkes Rich Cut Glass Works, 1889; D. 30.5 cm, Coll: Lightner Museum, St. Augustine, Florida, Gift of Samuel Hawkes. (Corning only)

45. *Place setting, cut in "Russian" pattern.* T.G. Hawkes & Co., ca. 1882-1900; H. (tallest goblet) 15.8 cm, The Corning Museum of Glass, Gift of Miss F. Ethel Wickham (57.4.9A-G). [Fig. 30]

46. *Plate, cut in "Russian" pattern.* T.G. Hawkes & Co., ca. 1906; D. 34 cm, The Corning Museum of Glass, Gift of T.G. Hawkes & Co. (51.4.536). [Fig. 41]

47. *Cut bowl.* T.G. Hawkes & Co., 1909; H. 8.4 cm, Coll: Miss Evelyn and Miss Mildred Durkin. [Fig. 44]

48. *Lamp, cut in "Queen's" pattern.* T.G. Hawkes & Co., ca. 1900-1915; H. 40.6 cm, Coll: Mr. and Mrs. Jay Doros. [Fig. 42]

49. *Cut round tray.* T.G. Hawkes & Co., ca. 1900-1915; D. 38.1 cm, Coll: Harry Kraut. [Fig. 45]

50. *Cut plate.* T.G. Hawkes & Co., ca. 1900-1915; D. 33.3 cm, The Corning Museum of Glass, Gift of R. Lee Waterman (76.4.50). [Fig. 43]

51. *Cut urn.* T.G. Hawkes & Co., ca. 1900-1915; H. 30.5 cm, Coll: Museum of Glass, Wheaton Historical Association, Millville, New Jersey, Gift of Mrs. Estelle Sinclaire Farrar. [Fig. 46]

52. *Bowl, engraved in "rock crystal" style.* T.G. Hawkes & Co., ca. 1920's; D. 20.3 cm, Coll: Mrs. Estelle Sinclaire Farrar. [Fig. 36]

53. *Wineglass, stone engraved in "Gravic Iris" pattern.* T.G. Hawkes & Co., ca. 1902-1940; H. 13.3 cm, The Corning Museum of Glass (74.4.172). [Fig. 90]

54. *Green banded wineglass.* T.G. Hawkes & Co., ca. 1920-1933; H. 13.2 cm, Coll: Robert F. Rockwell III. [Fig. 93]

55. *Ruby cased over amber wineglass.* T.G. Hawkes & Co., ca. 1903-1940; H. 11.5 cm, Coll: Mrs. Penrose Hawkes. [Fig. 94]

56. *Three cut and engraved sample goblets.* T.G. Hawkes & Co., ca. 1940-1960; H. 19.3, 19.4, 19.6 cm, The Corning Museum of Glass, Gift of R. Lee Waterman (76.4.54; 76.4.55; 76.4.57). [Fig. 99 A, B, C]

57. *Cut wineglass* in the pattern ordered by President F.D. Roosevelt for the White House, T.G. Hawkes & Co., 1938; H. 15.5 cm, The Corning Museum of Glass, Gift of T.G. Hawkes & Co. (51.4.534). [Fig. 98]

THE O.F. EGGINTON CO., 1896-1918
HUNT GLASS WORKS, 1895-1972

58. *Vase, cut in "Calvé" pattern.* The O.F. Egginton Co., ca. 1895-1918; H. 17.6 cm, Coll: Miss Lucille Egginton and Mrs. Susan Egginton Altonen. (Corning only)

59. *Lamp, cut in "Virginia" pattern.* The O.F. Egginton Co., ca. 1896-1918; H. 36.7 cm, Coll: Arkansas Commemorative Commission, Little Rock, Arkansas (76B269). [Fig. 51]

60. *Celery tray, cut in "Trellis" pattern.* The O.F. Egginton Co., 1908-1918; L. 28 cm, Coll: Arkansas Commemorative Commission, Little Rock, Arkansas (76B189). [Fig. 49]

61. *Compote, cut in "Strathmore" pattern.* The O.F. Egginton Co., ca. 1896-1918; H. 20.9 cm, Coll: Arkansas Commemorative Commission, Little Rock, Arkansas (76B95). [Fig. 50]

62. *Cut and engraved vase.* Hunt & Sullivan, ca. 1900; H. 46.4 cm, Coll: Mrs. Dorothy Hunt Sullivan. (Corning only)

63. *Pair of engraved decanters in "rock crystal" style.* Hunt & Sullivan, or Hunt Glass Works, ca. 1900-1915; H. 32.9 cm and 33.1 cm, Coll: Mrs. Dorothy Hunt Sullivan. (Corning only)

64. *Bowl, cut in "Royal" pattern.* Hunt Glass Works, ca. 1911-1930; D. 24 cm, Coll: Robert F. Rockwell III. [Fig. 47]

65. *Vase, cut in a "Waterford" pattern.* Hunt Glass Works, ca. 1910-1930; H. 17.2 cm, Coll: Miss Mary Krebs. (Corning only)

66. *Jug.* Hunt Glass Works, cut by Lee Carr and engraved by Joseph Libisch on a Pairpoint blank, ca. 1915; H. 34.3 cm, The Corning Museum of Glass, Gift of D.J. and Russell Carr (62.4.40). [Fig. 48]

67. *Frame.* Hunt Glass Works, engraved by Nicholas Undereiner, ca. 1930-1935; H. 18.6 cm, Coll: Nicholas Williams. [Fig. 96]

68. *Cocktail shaker, engraved in "Elegance" pattern.* Hunt Glass Works ca. 1930-1940; H. 36 cm, The Corning Museum of Glass, Gift of Hunt Glass Works, Inc. (51.4.547). [Fig. 97]

STEUBEN GLASS WORKS, 1903-1918
STEUBEN GLASS, CORNING GLASS WORKS, 1918-1932
STEUBEN GLASS, INC., 1933

69. *Cut plate.* Steuben Glass Works, ca. 1903-1918; D. 44.6 cm, The Corning Museum of Glass, Gift of Otto Hilbert (74.4.173). [Fig. 52]

70. *Cut and engraved ewer in "rock crystal" style.* Steuben Glass Works, ca. 1904-1912; H. 26.4 cm, The Corning Museum of Glass, Gift of Mr. and Mrs. Gillett Welles (69.4.275). [Fig. 53]

71. *Cut console set, in "Alexandrite" glass.* Steuben Glass, Corning Glass Works, 1920's; H. of candlesticks 30.5 and 30.8 cm, Coll: The Rockwell-Corning Museum. [Fig. 54]

72. *Ruby cased place setting* engraved for L.P. Fisher by Joseph Libisch. Steuben Glass, Corning Glass Works, 1920's; H. of tallest glass 25.3 cm, Coll: The Rockwell-Corning Museum. [Fig. 55]

73. *Cut paperweight cologne with enclosed "Cintra" decoration.* Steuben Glass, Corning Glass Works, 1920's; H. 22.5 cm, The Corning Museum of Glass, Gift of Otto Hilbert (75.4.61). [Fig. 56]

74. *Cut covered bowl, "Moonlight" glass.* Steuben Glass, Corning Glass Works, 1920's; H. 38.1 cm, Coll: The Rockwell-Corning Museum. [Fig. 57]

75. *Urn, engraved in "Strawberry Mansion" pattern.* Steuben Glass, Corning Glass Works, ca. 1932; H. 32.6 cm, Coll: The Rockwell-Corning Museum. [Fig. 58]

H.P. SINCLAIRE & CO., 1904-1928

76. *Decanter, cut and engraved in "Birds, Bees and Flowers" pattern.* H.P. Sinclaire & Co., ca. 1905-1928; H. 33.7 cm, The Corning Museum of Glass, Gift of Mrs. John Sinclaire (63.4.19). [Fig. 60]

77. *Cologne, engraved in "Figures" pattern.* H.P. Sinclaire & Co., ca. 1905-1928; H. 19.5 cm, Private Collection. (Corning only)

78. *Tray, cut in "Assyrian" pattern.* H.P. Sinclaire & Co., ca. 1909-1918; L. 30.5 cm, Coll: Mrs. Estelle Sinclaire Farrar. [Fig. 59]

79. *Three cut goblets.* H.P. Sinclaire & Co., 1905-1918; H. of tallest 16.5 cm, Coll: Mrs. Philip Willis. (Corning only)

80. *Green cased rose jar,* designed and engraved for Mrs. H.P. Sinclaire, Sr., H.P. Sinclaire & Co., 1927; H. 20.4 cm, Private Collection. (Corning only)

81. *Cut and stone-engraved punch bowl.* H.P. Sinclaire & Co., ca. 1905-1918; H. 38.7 cm, Coll: Harry Kraut. [Fig. 61]

82. *Iced tea glass, engraved in "rock crystal" style.* H.P. Sinclaire & Co., 1905-1927; H. 14.8 cm, Private Collection. (Corning only)

83. *Cologne, engraved in "Pillars and Roses" pattern.* H.P. Sinclaire & Co., 1905-1927; H. 18.2 cm, Coll: Mrs. Estelle Sinclaire Farrar. [Fig. 62]

84. *Plate, engraved in "Deer" pattern.* H.P. Sinclaire & Co., ca. 1905-1918; D. 25.3 cm, Coll: Mrs. Percy Orr. (Corning only)

85. *Blue banded finger bowl and plate, cut and engraved.* H.P. Sinclaire & Co., ca. 1920's; D. of plate 16.4 cm, Coll: Mr. and Mrs. John Marx. [Fig. 95]

86. *Blue banded wineglass and iced tea glass, cut and engraved.* H.P. Sinclaire & Co., 1920's; H. of wineglass 13.4 cm, Coll: Mrs. Estelle Sinclaire Farrar. [Fig. 95]

SMALLER FIRMS, 1894-1930

87. *Cut bowl.* Joseph Wilson & Sons, ca. 1894-1897; D. 20.5 cm, The Corning Museum of Glass (74.4.143). [Fig. 63]

88. *Cut bowl.* Almy & Thomas, ca. 1903-1907; D. 20.3 cm, The Corning Museum of Glass (57.4.21). [Fig. 64]

89. *Bowl.* Standard Cut Glass Company, cut by Samuel T. Share, 1905-1908; D. 21.5 cm, Coll: Miss A.E. McCloskey. [Fig. 65]

90. *Two cut nappies.* Painter cut glass shop, 1904-1905; D. 12.7 cm, 12.8 cm (handled), Coll: Mrs. Louise H. Hallahan. [Fig. 66]

91. *Green cased bowl.* Giometti Brothers, cut by Clarence Giometti; ca. 1903-1920; D. 16.1 cm, Coll: Mrs. Louise Giometti Smith. [Fig. 67]

92. *Cut lamp.* Giometti Brothers, ca. 1903-1920; H. 45.3 cm, Coll: Mrs. Matthew W. Cammen. [Fig. 68]

93. *Cut decanter and tumbler.* Majestic Cut Glass Company, ca. 1900-1910; H. of decanter 30.2 cm, Coll: Mrs. Beatrice Perling. [Fig. 69]

94. *Cut finger bowl and plate.* Majestic Cut Glass Company, ca. 1900-1910; D. of plate 16.2 cm, Coll: Mrs. Beatrice Perling. [Fig. 69]

95. *Cut compote.* Eygabroat-Ryon Company or Stage-Kashins Cut Glass Company, cut by Everett Stage, ca. 1910; H. 25.2 cm, Coll: Mrs. Adeline Stage Butla. [Fig. 70]

96. *Stone-engraved tray.* H.P. Sinclaire & Co., probably engraved by John N. Illig, ca. 1906-1915; L. 36 cm, Coll: Mrs. Estelle Sinclaire Farrar. [Fig. 86]

97. *Cut and engraved clock.* John N. Illig, Manufacturer of Artistically Engraved Glassware, 1920's; H. 16.5 cm, Coll: Mrs. E.J. Illig. [Fig. 88]

98. *Cut and engraved pitcher.* John N. Illig, Manufacturer of Artistically Engraved Glassware, 1920's; H. 17.2 cm, Coll: Mrs. Virginia Illig Driscoll. [Fig. 88]

99. *Plate.* Cut by Peter A. Eick, ca. 1912-1920; D. 30.5 cm, Coll: Miss Florence and Miss Evelyn Eick. (Corning only)

100. *Cased amber cut plate.* Fred Fuller, Cut Glass Manufacturer, ca. 1915; D. 28.1 cm, Coll: Mrs. Emil Schrickel. [Fig. 92]

101. *Cut punch bowl.* Ideal Cut Glass Co., Canastota, New York, ca. 1915; H. 32. cm, Coll: Mr. and Mrs. John Jeppson. [Fig. 71]

TUTHILL CUT GLASS COMPANY, MIDDLETOWN, NEW YORK, 1900-1923

102. *Lamp, cut in "Rex" pattern.* Tuthill Cut Glass Company, Middletown, New York, 1900-1923; H. 56.9 cm, Coll: Mrs. Freda Lipkowitz. [Fig. 72]

103. *Cut and stone-engraved punch bowl set, "Vintage" pattern.* Tuthill Cut Glass Company, Middletown, New York, ca. 1900-1923; H. 41.2 cm, The Corning Museum of Glass, Gift of Bernice Van Yorx Wickham (71.4.117). [Fig. 73]

104. *Bowl.* Tuthill Cut Glass Company, Middletown, New York, stone-engraved and cut by Leon Swope, ca. 1912; D. 22.9 cm, Coll: Leon Swope. [Fig. 74]

CORNING ENGRAVERS

105. *Ewer.* Thomas Webb & Sons, Stourbridge, England, designed and engraved in "rock crystal" style by William Fritsche, 1886; H. 38.5 cm, The Corning Museum of Glass (54.2.16). [Fig. 32]

106. *Vase,* exhibited at the Paris Exposition of 1889. Hawkes Rich Cut Glass Co., designed by H.P. Sinclaire, Jr., engraved by Joseph Haselbauer, 1889. This design was manufactured by H.P. Sinclaire & Co., 1904-1928. H. 33.8 cm, The Corning Museum of Glass, Gift of Mrs. John Sinclaire (63.4.20). [Fig. 34]

107. *Pair of vases.* Designed, cut, and engraved by Frederick and George Haselbauer, ca. 1911-1920; H. 40 cm and 39.8 cm, Coll: Mrs. Catherine Haselbauer Dencenburg. [Fig. 80]

108. *Vase.* Designed, cut, and engraved by George Haselbauer, ca. 1911-1920; H. 30.6 cm, Coll: Mrs. Catherine Haselbauer Dencenburg. [Fig. 81]

109. *Pitcher.* Designed and engraved with portraits of President and Mrs. William McKinley by Hieronimus William Fritchie, ca. 1901; H. 25.6 cm, The Corning Museum of Glass, Gift of Mrs. Helen Fritchie Arnoldy (76.4.43). [Fig. 78]

110. *Decanter.* Designed and engraved by Joseph Nitsche, ca. 1893-1900; H. 26.4 cm, Coll: Mrs. Grace Nitsche Barker. [Fig. 75]

111. *Tray, in "Rich Carnation" pattern.* Designed and engraved by Clement Nitsche for H.P. Sinclaire & Co., ca. 1915; L. 29.3 cm, Coll: Mrs. Estelle Sinclaire Farrar. [Fig. 76]

112. *Three sample goblets.* Designed and engraved by Adolf Kretschmann, ca. 1920-1940; H. 15.3 cm, 15.8 cm, 17.3 cm, Coll: Mrs. Esther Kretschmann Patch. [Fig. 91]

113. *Pitcher, "Before the Storm."* Designed and engraved by Edward Palme, ca. 1900-1910; H. 25.2 cm, Coll: Mrs. Edward J. Palme, Jr. [Fig. 83]

114. *Vase.* Designed and engraved by Ernest Kaulfuss, 1930's; H. 27.2 cm, Coll: Mrs. Dorothy Kaulfuss Coats. [Fig. 82]

115. *Pitcher.*Designed and engraved by Hiram Rouse with a self-portrait, ca. 1905; H. 24.5 cm, Coll: Mrs. Jennifer Jacoby Dawson. [Fig. 79]

116. *Pitcher.* Designed and engraved by Wilmot Putnam, ca. 1910-1920; H. 11.6 cm, Coll: Wilmot L. Putnam, Jr. [Fig. 77]

117. *Vase.* Engraved by John N. Illig on a broken and salvaged Sinclaire blank, 1905; H. 19.3 cm, Coll: Mrs. Mary Illig. [Fig. 87]

118. *Blue vase.* Designed and engraved by Joseph Libisch on a Sinclaire blank, 1930's; H. 27.9 cm, Coll: Mrs. Estelle Sinclaire Farrar. [Fig. 84]

119. *Vase, "Kingfishers."* Designed and engraved by Joseph Libisch, 1930's; H. 25.1 cm, Coll: Mrs. Helen Libisch Elmer. [Fig. 85]

120. *Gazelle bowl.* Steuben Glass, Inc., designed by Sidney Waugh, engraved by Joseph Libisch, 1935; D. 16.5 cm, Coll: The Metropolitan Museum of Art, New York City, Fund of Edward C. Moore (35.94.1). [Fig. 100]

121. *Bowl.* T.G. Hawkes & Co., designed and engraved by William Morse, 1920's; D. 20.3 cm, Coll: Mrs. Sheldon Smith.

COLLEAGUES AND COMPETITORS

122. *Cut lamp.* C. Dorflinger & Sons, ca. 1880's; H. 67.3 cm, Coll: Harry Kraut. [Fig. 101]

123. *Cut vase.* C. Dorflinger & Sons, ca. 1880's; H. 31.5 cm, Ex. Coll: Louis Dorflinger; The Corning Museum of Glass, Gift of Kathryn Dorflinger Manchee (71.4.126). [Fig. 102]

124. *Cut wineglass.* C. Dorflinger & Sons, ca. 1890's; H. 11.5 cm, The Corning Museum of Glass, Gift of Kathryn Dorflinger Manchee (71.4.123). [Fig. 104]

125. *Green cased punch bowl set, cut in "Montrose" pattern.* C. Dorflinger & Sons, ca. 1895; D. 33 cm, Coll: Harry Kraut. [Fig. 103]

126. *Ruby cased wineglasses* like those in a set ordered by the Prince of Wales during his American tour. C. Dorflinger & Sons, ca. 1918; H. 12.1 cm, The Corning Museum of Glass, Gift of Kathryn Dorflinger Manchee (71.4.124). [Fig. 105]

127. *Punch bowl set* engraved for The World's Columbian Exposition, Chicago. Libbey Glass Company, ca. 1892; H. H. 34.3 cm, Coll: The Toledo Museum of Art, Toledo, Ohio, Gift of the Libbey Glass Company (15.16). [Fig. 106]

128. *Lamp, cut in "Ellesmere" pattern,* for The World's Columbian Exposition, Chicago. Libbey Glass Company, 1893; H. 83.8 cm, Coll: The Toledo Museum of Art, Toledo, Ohio, Gift of Owens-Illinois, Inc. (51.2). [Fig. 107]

129. *Punch bowl set,* duplicate of one cut for President McKinley. Libbey Glass Company, 1898; D. 45.7 cm, Coll: Carl U. Fauster. [Fig. 108]

130. *Plate, "Apotheosis of Transportation,"* engraved for the Louisiana Purchase Exposition, St. Louis, Libbey Glass Company, 1904: D. 31.1 cm, Coll: Smithsonian Institution, Washington, D.C. (236.934). [Fig. 109]

131. *Engraved plaque showing glass cutting.* Libbey Glass Company, 1905; D. 23.8 cm, Coll: Smithsonian Institution, Washington, D.C. (236.924). [Fig. 110]

132. *Engraved plaque showing glass engraving.* Libbey Glass Company, 1905; D. 23.8 cm, Coll: Smithsonian Institution, Washington, D.C. (236.926). [Fig. 111]

133. *Punchbowl on stand.* Cut for the Lewis and Clark Exposition, Portland, Oregon. H.C. Fry Glass Company, 1905; H. 137 cm, Coll: Mr. and Mrs. Philip Roberts. [Fig. 112]

134. *Lamp.* Probably cut by L. Straus & Sons for The World's Columbian Exposition, Chicago, 1893; H. 3.658 m, Coll: Milton Hershey School, Hershey, Pennsylvania. (Corning only)

Cutting And Engraving Companies And Home Shops
Corning, New York, 1868-1940

*A Chronological List**

HOARE & DAILEY, LATER J. HOARE & CO.
  Cut and engraved glass.
  1868-1915: Corning Glass Works Bldg. No. 1, foot of Walnut St.
  1915-1920: 56-58 Bridge St.

  Branch shops: southeast corner, Cedar St. and Tioga Ave., 1901-1904.
  Wellsboro, Pa., 1906-1908.

  Acid-stamped trade mark, "J. Hoare & Co., 1853, Corning, N.Y."
  1890-1920, HOARE acid-stamped on stemware.

JOSEPH F. HASELBAUER
  Engraving subcontractor.[1]
  1873-1893: address unknown.
  1893-1910: 84 W. Third St.

HAWKES RICH CUT GLASS CO., LATER T.G. HAWKES & CO.
  Cut and engraved glass.
  1880-1883: Market St., number unknown.
  1883-1962: 77 W. Market St.

  Branch shops: two on Erie Ave., ca. 1900-after 1910.
  Subsidiary: Steuben Glass Works, 1903-1918.

  Sticker trade mark, two hawks and fleur-de-lis above the name
  Hawkes, 1890-ca. 1899. The same, acid-stamped, ca. 1899-1962.
  The same with "Gravic Glass," "Hawkes Gravic" added 1901-1962.
  HAWKES acid-stamped on stemware.

HIERONIMUS WILLIAM FRITCHIE
  Engraving subcontractor.
  1904-1916: head of Walnut St.
  Some work signed "H.W. Fritchie" in diamond-point script.

JOSEPH NITSCHE, CLEMENT NITSCHE
  Engraving subcontractors. ca. 1893-1937: Rear of 138 W. Fifth St.

FRANK WILSON & SONS
  Cutting subcontractors for Bawo & Dotter, New York City.
  1894-ca. 1897: 19 Sly Ave.
  (No trade mark known)

HUNT & SULLIVAN, LATER HUNT GLASS WORKS; HUNT GLASS WORKS, INC.
  Cut and engraved glass.
  1895-1948: 196 W. Sixth St.
  1948-ca. 1972: 300 E. Third St.

  Acid-stamped script "Hunt" from before 1906 to ca. 1915;
  thereafter, the same trade mark was used on stickers for
  an indefinite period.

THE O.F. EGGINTON CO., ALSO CALLED EGGINTON RICH CUT GLASS WORKS.
  Cut glass.
  1896-1918: 152-174 W. Fifth St.

  Acid-stamped trade mark incorporating the name Egginton.

GEORGE W. DRAKE & CO.
  Cut glass.
  Ca. 1899-1901: rear of 52 E. Fifth St.
  1901-1908: 56-58 Bridge St.
  No trade mark known.

JOSEPH BLACKBURN
Cutting subcontractor.
1901-1905: 300 Baker St.

ERNEST MULFORD
Cutting subcontractor.
1901-ca. 1911: 94 John St.

ARCADIAN CUT GLASS CO.
A trade journal reported this company in Corning in 1902.
There is no trace of it in Corning records, but near-
invisibility was the rule, rather than the exception, for
branch shops of out-of-town companies.

CORNING CUT GLASS CO.
Cut glass.
1901-ca. 1911: Hart Ave., Riverside; office at 2 W. Erie Ave.,
    Corning.
"Corning Cut Glass Co., Corning, N.Y." acid-stamped for a
very brief period; thereafter, "C.C.G."

KNICKERBOCKER CUT GLASS CO.
Product unknown.
1902-1903: 63 E. Erie Ave.
No trade mark known.

GIOMETTI BROTHERS
Cut glass.
1902-1907 and 1909-1933: 205 W. Water St.
1907-1909: in Watkins Glen, N.Y.
No trade mark known.

PATRICK CALLAHAN
One-man cutting shop.
Ca. 1902-ca. 1916: rear of 73 W. Fourth St.
No signature known.

ALMY & THOMAS
Cut glass.
1903-1907: 63 E. Erie Ave.
Acid-stamped cipher of the letters A and T.

ELMIRA CUT GLASS CO.
Cut glass.
Branch shop of the Elmira company until 1910 ; bought by
J. Hoare & Co. 1913.
1903-1910: Address unknown.
1910-1913; 63 E. Erie Ave.
1913-1914: foot of Walnut St.
No trade mark known.

STEUBEN GLASS WORKS; LATER STEUBEN DIVISION, CORNING GLASS
WORKS; NOW STEUBEN GLASS.[2]
Cut and engraved glass.
1903-1937; W. Erie Ave.
1933-1951; factory in Corning Glass Works. Offices in New York City.
1951-to date: Corning Glass Center.
Acid-stamped trefoil with fleur-de-lis and name STEUBEN occasionally
acid-stamped on stemware. After 1933, diamond-point script "S"
or "Steuben."

IDEAL CUT GLASS CO.
1903-1905: rear of 75 W. Pulteney St.
1905-1933: in Canastota, N.Y.
No trade mark known.

EMIL WALTER
Engraving subcontractor.
Ca. 1904-ca. 1935: 161 W. Fourth St.
No signature known.

PAINTER CUT GLASS SHOP (FORMAL NAME, IF ANY, UNKNOWN).
Cut glass.
1904-ca. 1905: Rear of 36 E. Market St.
No trade mark known.

H.P. SINCLAIRE & CO.
Cut and engraved glass.[3]
1904-1928: Conhocton St. from Erie Ave. to East Market Street.
Acid-stamped S in wreath. SINCLAIRE acid-stamped on
stemware.

ERNEST L. BRADLEY
Product unknown.
Ca. 1904-1906: 134 W. Tioga Ave.
Trade mark unknown.

STANDARD CUT GLASS CO.
Cut glass.
This company may have been a branch shop of an out-of-town
company.
1905-1908: on W. Market St. (number unknown), at 63 E. Erie
Ave., and at 136 w. Tioga Ave.
No trade mark known.

DELOS V. OLIN
Cutting subcontractor.
1906-?: 136 Myrtle Ave.

AUGUSTUS K. ROSE
Cutting subcontractor.
1907-?: Main St., Gibson.

MAJESTIC CUT GLASS CO.
Cut glass.
Branch shop of the Elmira Company.
Ca. 1907-ca. 1911: address unknown.
No trade mark known.

EDWARD PALME, SR.
Engraving subcontractor.
1907-ca. 1940 264 W. Second St.
No signature known.

EYGABROAT-RYON
Cut glass.
Branch shop of the Lawrenceville, Pa., company.
Ca. 1908-ca. 1909: 63 E. Erie Ave.
No trade mark known.

ERNEST KAULFUSS
Engraving subcontractor.
1908-ca. 1948: chiefly at 48 Conhocton St.

HENRY KELLER
Engraving subcontractor.
Ca. 1909-1912: 337 E. First st.
1912-1950: 376 Watauga Ave.

HIRAM ROUSE
Engraving subcontractor.
Ca. 1910-1960's: rear of 237 Chestnut St.

J.F. HASELBAUER & SONS, MANUFACTURERS OF RICH ROCK
CRYSTAL AND ENGRAVED WARE
 Also cut-and-engraved glass.
 1910-1938: 84 W. Third St.
 No trade mark known.

JOSEPH LIBISCH
 Engraving subcontractor.
 1921-1924: 109 W. Market St.
 1924-1937: southeast corner of Dodge Ave. and Pulteney St.

THOMAS SHOTTEN CUT GLASS CO. (ALSO SPELLED SHOTTON)
 Cut glass.
 1912: two factories, at 56-58 Bridge St. and the southeast
 corner of Cedar St. and Tioga Ave.
 No trade mark known.

PETER A. EICK
 Cut glass.[4]
 1912-1935: 131 W. Fifth St.
 No signature known.

SIGNET GLASS CO.
 Possibly a Hawkes subsidiary.
 Type of decoration unknown but inexpensive.
 1913-1928 or earlier: address unknown.
 No trade mark known.

JOHN N. ILLIG, MANUFACTURER OF ARTISTICALLY ENGRAVED
GLASSWARE.
 1915-1917: 136 W. Tioga Ave.
 1917-1921: 227 E. Market St.
 1921-ca. 1929: 152-174 W. Fifth St.
 No trade mark known.

HARRY M. JONES
 One-man cutting shop.
 Ca. 1915-ca. 1925: rear of 210 W. Second St.
 No signature known.

FRED H. FULLER, CUT GLASS MANUFACTURER
 Only intaglio cuttings on inexpensive blanks are known.
 Ca. 1916-ca. 1927: Washington St., outside city limits.
 No trade mark known.

PETER KAULFUSS
 One-man engraving shop.
 Ca. 1918-ca. 1926: 160 Steuben St.
 No signature known.

ADOLF KRETSCHMANN
 Engraving subcontractor.
 Ca. 1918-1955: 345 W. First St.

BENJAMIN R. WATSON
 Chiefly cut glass; some engraving.
 Ca. 1920-ca. 1941: 164 Columbia St.
 Watson sometimes worked his first and last initials into the
 design of his engraved glass.

AMBROSE VAN ETTEN
 One-man cutting shop.
 Ca. 1920-1953, with several interruptions: in Gibson and
 Horseheads, N.Y.
 No signature known.

WILMOT PUTNAM
Engraving subcontractor.
Ca. 1920-1969: 202 Baker St.

ANTHONY KELLER, SR.
Engraving shop.
Ca. 1920-ca. 1930: 228 E. Market St.
No signature known.

DENSON & COSGROVE
Subcontractors, chiefly of stoppering for Steuben.
Early 1920: barn behind Robinson's grocery store, Gibson.
Ca. 1925-ca. 1930: 270 E. Third St., Corning.

JOSEPH HAHNE
One-man engraving shop.
Ca. 1925-ca. 1940; 60 W. Third St.
No signature known.

HARRY GOODMAN
Jewelry cut from glass and engraved.
1925-1931: 26 W. Market St.
no signature known.

EDWARD PALME, JR.
Engraving subcontractor.
Ca. 1925-1968: 91 W. Third St.

JOSEPH OVESZNY (ALSO SPELLED OVESNEY, OVESCNY)
Engraved glass.
Ca. 1930-1942 (except for about a year away from Corning):
24 E. Fourth St.
No signature known.

AIDEN JOHNSON
Engraving subcontractor.
1930's-1968: 24 W. Sixth St.

FRANK KONIGSTEIN & EDWARD HAUPTMANN
Engraved glass.
Ca. 1933-ca., 1951: Rose Hill, R.d. #2. Konigstein may have
continued alone after 1951.

FLOYD MANWARREN
Cutting subcontractor and repair shop.
1939-1945, Beaver Dams, N.Y.
1945-to date: Watkins Road.
No signature.

*List includes the contiguous villages of Riverside and Gibson. Cutters and engravers who worked at home only occasionally have been omitted.

1. Subcontractors also worked for private customers, but did not sign their work. H.W. Fritchie is the only known exception, and his signature is rare.

2. For a full account of art glass made by Steuben from 1903-1933, see Gardner, Paul V. *The Glass of Frederick Carder.* New York: Crown Publishers, Inc., 1971.

3. For a full account of the company's art glass see Farrar, Estelle Sinclaire. *H.P. Sinclaire, Jr., Glassmaker.* 2 vols. Garden City, N.Y.: Farrar Books, 1974-1975.

4. Corningites remember that Eick "engraved" some of the Pyrex teapots that were popular in the Twenties. Virtually all were in fact intaglio cut, including Eick's.

Corning Firms That Have been Incorrectly Identified

REPORTED NAME	PROBABLE EXPLANATION
Allen Cut Glass Co.	J. Hoare & Co. Branch shop, run by a cutter named Allen.
Black, Joseph	Joseph Blackburn.
Climax Cut Glass Co.	A name considered for Elmira Cut Glass Co.'s Corning shop.
Crystal City Cut Glass Co.	George W. Drake considered using this name. James O. Sebring also considered it for his Corning Cut Glass Co.
Crystal Glass Co.	James Sebring considered this name for a blank-manufacturing company that never opened.
Ferris Cut Glass Co.	Elmira Cut Glass Co., owned by the Ferris brothers.
Holton Glass Co.	Possibly a Corning branch of Stage Brothers, whose foreman was William Holton.
Imperial Cut Glass Co.	Considered as a name for Ideal Cut Glass Co.
Sebring Brothers Sebring Cut Glass Co.	Popular nicknames for James Sebring's Corning Cut Glass Co.
Wellsboro Cut Glass Co.	John Hoare, Inc., Wellsboro, Pa.

Bibliography

The Aristocratic Journey, Being the Outspoken Letters of Mrs. Basil Hall Written during a Fourteen Months' Sojourn in America, 1827-1828. Ed. Una Pope-Hennessy. New York: Putnam and Sons, 1931.

Baron Klinkowstrom's America, 1818-1820. First ed. Stockholm 1824. Tr. and ed. Franklin D. Scott. Evanston: Northwestern University Press, 1952.

Boston Daily Evening Transcript, March 13, 1835.

Boston Daily Journal, Feb. 26, 1850.

Columbian Centinel, Boston, Mass., Oct. 15, 1835, p. 1, col. 3.

Corning Journal, 1868-1920.

Dorflinger, William F. "The Development of the Cut Glass Business in the United States." Paper read before the American Association of Flint and Lime Glass Manufacturers at the Annual Meeting at Atlantic City, N.J., July 25, 1902.

Eastern Argus. Portland, Maine, March 28, 1825.

Elville, E.M. *English and Irish Cut Glass, 1750-1950.* London: Country Life Ltd., 1953.

Fearon, Henry Bradshaw. *Sketches of America. A Narrative of a Journey of Five Thousand Miles through the Eastern and Western States of America* ... 2nd ed. London: printed for Longman, Hurst, Rees, Orme, and Brown, 1818.

Fordham, Elias Pym. *Personal Narrative of Travels in Virginia, Maryland, Pennsylvania, Ohio, Indiana, Kentucky; and of a Residence in the Illinois Territory: 1817-1818.* Ed. F.A. Ogg. Cleveland: Arthur H. Clark Company, 1906.

Innes, Lowell. *Pittsburgh Glass, 1797-1891, A History and Guide for Collectors.* Boston: Houghton-Mifflin, 1976.

Letter to Mr. Niles of the Baltimore *Weekly Register,* Aug. 30, 1819, cited by Hortense F. Sicard, "Glassmaker to Two Presidents," *Antiques,* 25, no. 2., 1934.

McKearin, George S. and Helen. *American Glass.* New York: Crown Publishers, Inc., 1941.

Manufacturers' and Farmers Journal, Providence and Pawtucket Advertiser, November 29, 1821.

Nevins, Allan. *American Social History as Recorded by British Travellers.* New York: Henry Holt and Co., 1931.

Papers on Appeal, p. 304, Record, Corning Glass Works *v.* Corning Cut Glass Company *et al.,* 126 A.D. 919, 75 A.D. 629 (Fourth Dept., 1902).

Pittsburgh Mercury. Nov. 10, 1818, cited by Thomas C. Pears, Jr. "The First Successful Flint Glass Factory in America ...," *Antiques,* 11, no. 3, 1927.

Title page, *The Western Address Directory.* Baltimore: printed by Jos. Robinson, 1837.